Notable Women

Arlene J. Morris-Lipsman

Illustrations by Mary Crisanti

SCOTT, FORESMAN AND COMPANY
GLENVIEW, ILLINOIS   LONDON

Good Year Books
are available for preschool through grade 12 and for
every basic curriculum subject plus many enrichment
areas. For more Good Year Books, contact your local
bookseller or educational dealer. For a complete cata-
log with information about other Good Year Books,
please write:

Good Year Books
Department GYB
1900 East Lake Avenue
Glenview, Illinois 60025

1 2 3 4 5 6 VPI 94 93 92 91 90 89

ISBN 0-673-38743-7

To Ed
For your constant
and all-enduring
encouragement and support.
With love and gratitude,
A. J. M.-L.

PREFACE

The doors have opened wide for women. Where once a woman had only a few traditional career options, today all avenues of work are open to her. And for the most part, women are accepted, even welcomed, as they pursue their newly found rights to be whatever they wish.

But these changes did not come easily. Nor did they come quickly. While most women chose to wait out the struggle, a few individuals dared to aspire to glory and achievement. Their stories must be told, especially to children, for they can inspire young people to dream dreams of their own. This book examines the lives of several of these women.

Who are they, these notable women? They come from all over the world. Some belonged to the past. Some make today's front page news. Many of their names are known worldwide. Several of these women were the first in their fields. Their struggles to overcome the odds are superb lessons in determination and endurance. Others, while not the first, have greatly expanded our knowledge in a particular area or have achieved outstanding successes. Many of these women encountered some sort of prejudice because they were women. Despite it all, they continued until victory was theirs.

While their stories could fill pages, the selections in this book are brief, geared to hold the interest of students in the fourth through sixth grades. The information can be used to whet students' appetites and encourage them to read more about the women. It can also be used to motivate discussions about the youngsters' own goals and aspirations.

Several types of follow-up activities complement each narrative. Discussion questions based on each woman appear at the end of each selection. They go beyond mere facts, encouraging students to think, question, and imagine.

"Quotable Quotes" presents a quotation either by or about the individual with a follow-up question or two. These questions allow the students to study the woman further, and in so doing, learn more about her. To reinforce learning even further, students are often asked to supply their own quotations about the woman.

Two or three additional activities accompany each selection. Many of them reinforce key concepts. Some are designed to encourage children to think about the problems and prejudices the woman faced. Others ask the student to put themselves in the woman's place and decide for themselves how they would have solved her problems. All activities emphasize critical and creative thinking skills and involve written, oral, dramatic, or artistic projects.

Also included is an independent research section. This research will enable pupils to learn more about the woman and her contributions to society. Finally, a brief bibliography for further reading has been supplied to encourage children to read more about each woman.

Each major section of the book concludes with "Thinking It Over" activities that invite students to make comparisons and draw conclusions about the women studied in each section.

As a culminating activity, the students are asked to complete a chart regarding the women. As they fill in the chart, the students will be able to compare the lives of all these notable women, noting the similarities as well as the differences.

As the students read the material and complete the work pages, they will gain a better understanding of where women have been and how far they have come. Moreover, young girls and boys will learn that they, too, can set goals for themselves and aspire to be anything they want.

The author wishes to thank Anita Meinbach for her helpful reviews of the manuscript.

CONTENTS

POLITICS AND LAW

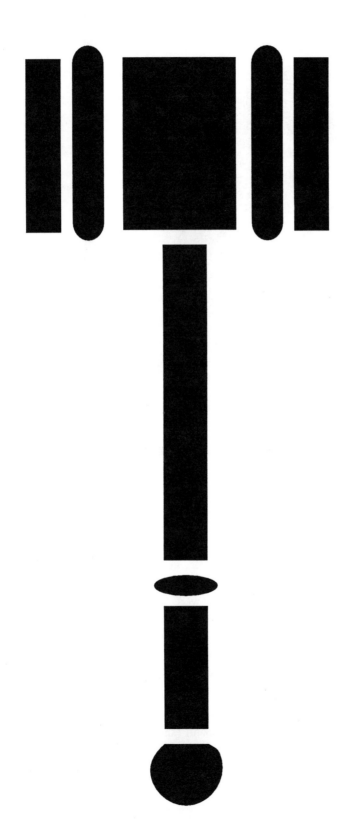

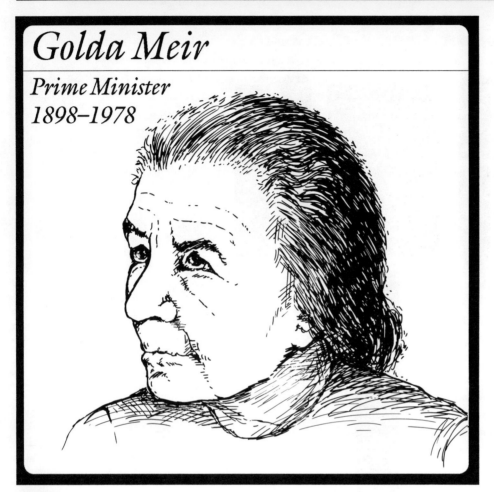

Golda Meir

Prime Minister
1898–1978

THROUGHOUT HER LIFETIME, Golda Meir had a dream to establish a new land. What part did she play in helping to make her dream come true?

Eight-year-old Golda Mabovitch breathed a happy sigh. At long last, she was in America. Living in Russia, Golda had worried about being beaten, even killed by her neighbors simply because she was a Jew. In America, she would not be afraid.

But what about the Jews living elsewhere in the world? They were often treated as badly as the Jews in Russia. And not all could go to America like Golda did.

More and more, Golda found herself believing that the Jewish people must have a state they could call their own—Palestine, the Jewish homeland of long ago. Although Great Britain now controlled Palestine, perhaps one day it would be an independent Jewish state. How Golda longed to be among the pioneers who were now leaving their countries, settling in Palestine, and developing the land.

Finally, in 1921, Golda made a decision. She and her husband (she had married Morris Myerson in 1917) left America and set sail for Palestine, in the Middle East.

For a while, Golda and Morris lived on a kibbutz, a large farm. But Morris was unhappy there, so to please him, Golda left the kibbutz she loved and moved to the city of Jerusalem.

For the next four years, Golda tried hard to be a good wife and mother. But home life was not enough for her. Desperately she wanted to help develop Palestine. Then Golda found what she was looking for. She began to work for the Histadrut, a large labor union that helped build roads, schools, and factories.

As time passed, Golda's responsibilities with the Histadrut grew, and she began to be recognized as a Jewish leader. She traveled to Europe and America, raising money for Palestine and talking to her fellow Jews about the need for a Jewish homeland.

Throughout the world, Jewish audiences listened to her and hoped her words would come true. For by now, German leader Adolf Hitler had declared war in Europe and was killing Jews by the millions. The Jews of Palestine were willing to take in the European Jews, but the British would not let them enter the country. And so, Golda joined with other Jewish leaders, smuggling their people in, protesting against the British, and begging world leaders for help.

When the war was over, the newly formed United Nations decided Palestine's fate. The country, the United Nations declared, would be divided into two states, one Arab (Arabs lived in Palestine along with the Jews), and one the Jewish state of Israel. On May 14, 1947 Golda Myerson and other Israeli officials proudly signed Israel's Proclamation of Independence.

Although Israel was now a state, Golda's work was not done. First she was chosen as Israel's ambassador (representative) to the Soviet Union. A few years later, in 1949, she became Israel's first minister of labor, and she developed programs to help immigrants settle in the land of Israel.

In 1956, Golda was asked to be Israel's foreign minister. Now she would be advising her government on matters that concerned Israel's place in the world. At that time she chose a Hebrew name for herself—Meir.

Golda Meir served her country until 1966. Nearly seventy, she decided to retire. In 1969, however, Israel's prime minister (leader of the country) died suddenly. Golda was asked to serve as prime minister until the fall elections. But that fall, the people chose Golda to continue leading the country.

As prime minister, Golda faced many serious challenges. In 1973, five neighboring Arab countries declared war on Israel once again. (Israel and her neighbors had fought several wars since 1947.) Golda was saddened by the war. Too many Jewish soldiers had lost their lives in battle.

After the brief war, Golda was once again elected prime minister. But a tired and sad Golda believed she could no longer serve her country. And so, in 1974, Golda Meir retired from public life. A few years later, in December 1978, she died.

For fifty years, she had worked for her people, placing their needs above her own. She had struggled and she had fought, but in the end, the battles had been won. Now rich, green fields had replaced the swamplands of Palestine. Gleaming cities rose above the sand. And even more, Jewish people were in charge of their own lives, their own destiny. Golda Meir had lived to see her dream come true. The state of Israel had been born.

FOR DISCUSSION

1. When Golda Meir lived in Russia, she lived in fear simply because she was Jewish. Jewish people throughout the world have often been mistreated by others. Why do you think this is so? How do you think having a homeland they could call their own would help the Jewish people?

2. Golda was happy living in America. Here she could live freely as a Jew. However, she longed to go to Palestine even though it was not yet a Jewish state. What might have motivated her desire to live in Palestine?

3. Although Golda tried to be a good wife and mother, home life was just not enough for her. What other things were of major importance in her life?

4. Even though Golda held many important positions in the Israeli government, she never even dreamed of the possibility that one day she would be prime minister. Why do you think she felt this way?

5. For many years Golda worked toward a dream and finally saw it come true. Israel had become a state. Instead of retiring at that point, Golda went on to work for the Israeli government until she was in her seventies. Think about the positions Golda held in the Israeli government. Identify some ways she could have continued to help the state of Israel grow and develop.

QUOTABLE QUOTES

Golda once wrote to her sister about her work and her separations from her family, "I ask only one thing. That I be understood and believed. My social activities are not an accidental thing. I am hurt when Morris and others say this is all superficial. That I am trying to be modern. You can understand how hard it is for me to leave. But in our present situation I could not refuse to do what was asked of me." What do these words tell you about the kind of conflicts Golda faced in her life?

ACTIVITIES

1. Golda Meir always hoped the day would come when Israel and its Arab neighbors would live together in peace. Imagine that this day has arrived and that Golda has lived to see it. The Arabs and Jews have just signed a peace treaty. All questions concerning who owns the land have been settled. What is left now is to ensure peace by furthering cooperation among the different peoples. To make sure that this happens, Golda has arranged for Israel and its neighbors to meet in a peace conference.

Imagine you are part of this peace conference. In your classroom, divide into small groups, representing the Arab countries of Egypt, Syria, and Lebanon as well as Israel and the Arabs who live inside Israel's borders. Within your groups, discuss ways that the Arabs and Israelis can work together for a lasting peace. For instance, perhaps a number of Israeli students can attend an Egyptian college to learn about Egypt's culture. What else can be done to spread cooperation and goodwill? List your ideas on a sheet of paper.

When the groups have completed their lists, arrange a peace conference among the groups. Select one student to present your group's ideas to the other nations. As each

group's list is presented, be prepared to comment on each idea. Do you think the ideas will work? How can they be put into effect?

When you have finished sharing your ideas, list them on the chalkboard. Decide which ones are the most important. Which should go into effect immediately?

2. The high point of Golda Meir's career came when she was chosen prime minister of Israel. Her entire life's occupations as well as her personality prepared her for this important position.

Think about each of the letters in the words "prime minister." On a sheet of paper, write the words vertically—going down the paper in a column. Next to each letter, write a word or phrase beginning with that letter describing Golda Meir as a person or something she did in her lifetime.

When you have finished, display the papers around the room so that the entire class can see each other's ideas.

FOR FURTHER RESEARCH

1. Find out more about Israel, the country Golda Meir dedicated her life to. By reading newspaper and magazine articles, learn about some of the problems Israel faces today, such as threats of war with her neighbors, how other major world powers view her, and how the Israeli people themselves accept their leaders' stands on issues. How are these problems similar to or different from the problems Golda faced when she served as prime minister?

2. When Golda Meir first settled in Palestine, she worked on a kibbutz. A kibbutz, which is really a large farm, represents a unique type of living arrangement. Find out how the kibbutz system works. Do we have anything similar to kibbutz life in the United States? Why do you think the kibbutz system works in Israel but does not work in the United States?

3. Golda Meir's first position for the newly formed state of Israel was that of ambassador to the Soviet Union. (In the United States we also send ambassadors to foreign countries.) Learn about what kinds of duties an ambassador performs. Why do you think Golda was chosen as ambassador to the Soviet Union? Why was it especially important to the government of Israel that Golda do her job well?

FOR FURTHER READING

Adler, David A. Our Golda: *The Story of Golda Meir*. New York: Viking Press, 1984.

Davidson, Margaret. *The Golda Meir Story*. New York: Charles Scribner's Sons, 1981.

Keller, Mollie. *Golda Meir*. New York: Franklin Watts, 1983.

Indira Gandhi

Prime Minister
1917–1984

NDIRA GANDHI BECAME A WELL-KNOWN AND RESPECTED international figure. Few other women in the world held the position Indira did. But with this great responsibility came tremendous problems. What obstacles did she face?

Life was often lonely for young Indira Nehru. Her beloved father, who was leading the fight for India's independence from Great Britain, was often in jail. And her mother was busy, too, protesting against the British.

How Indira longed to help her country. But she was only twelve, too young to join the Indian National Congress party, which was dedicated to fighting for India's freedom. Determined to do her part, Indira gathered over a thousand youngsters together and formed her own children's protest group, the Monkey Brigade. She and the other children eagerly aided their parents in their fight for freedom.

The years passed. Indira was now attending college in England, and her mother had died. But she soon grew homesick, and in 1941 she returned to India. At last, thought Indira, she was old enough to join the Congress party.

Eagerly she and her husband (she had married Feroze Gandhi in 1942) became involved in India's freedom movement. It wasn't long before Indira was arrested for organizing a public meeting. For thirteen months, Indira Gandhi remained in prison. Finally she was released.

More good news soon followed. In August 1947, India became an independent nation—and Indira's father was chosen as prime minister. He would now lead the country. How thrilled Indira was, and how proud she was of her father.

Indira quickly became her father's hostess and was recognized as first lady of the land. Even more, she accompanied her father on his many travels around the world. Quietly Indira listened as world leaders discussed policies with her father. Slowly she began to learn about world affairs.

As first lady, Indira was also concerned about many of India's problems. Wanting to help her people, she organized several welfare and educational programs. She also became involved in politics. She began to work for the Congress party, serving on some of its committees. In 1959, she was elected president of the party. She made many important decisions and proved that she was a strong leader.

In 1964, Indira's father became ill. She not only took care of him but helped run the country, too. When he died a few months later, the party considered Indira as the person to take his place.

But Indira Gandhi did not feel ready to be prime minister of India. Instead, she became minister of information and broadcasting for India's new prime minister, Lal Bahadur Shasti.

For two years she served Shasti, until he died. Once again, the party thought that Indira would be a good leader, and this time she accepted the position of prime minister.

Although some people wondered if she could do the job, Indira was determined to prove that she could lead India. She soon found out, though, how difficult the job could be. For India is a country with many problems—overpopulation, poverty, disease, and illiteracy are some.

Trying hard to make India the best country it could be, Indira led the government for the next several years. But then, in 1975, trouble arose. Indira had not won the last election fairly, people said. Some even wanted her to resign from office. But Indira didn't resign. Instead, she put many of her opponents in jail. This made many Indians even angrier, and in 1977 she lost the election for prime minister.

Indira refused to give up, however, and in 1980 she was once again chosen as India's leader.

These were not easy times for India. The Sikhs, a religious group of people who live in India, wanted to establish their own state. They often fought with their Indian neighbors, trying to achieve their aims. Angry about this fighting, Indira ordered her soldiers to attack the Sikh temple, killing many people. Of course the Sikhs were furious. Some even wanted revenge on Indira. And one day they got that revenge. Two of her own bodyguards (who were Sikhs) shot her as she walked through her garden. On October 31, 1984, Indira Gandhi died from her wounds.

It was a sad moment for the Indian people. Indira, they knew, had spent her lifetime working for her country. When so few countries dared to choose a woman leader, Indira was guiding India along, helping to make it a major world power. On her death, the Indian people thought about their leader. They would miss Indira Gandhi.

From *Notable Women*, by Arlene J. Morris-Lipsman, Copyright © 1990 Scott, Foresman and Company.

FOR DISCUSSION

1. Why do you think Indians were fighting for their independence from Britain? What other countries do you know about that have also fought for their independence? Do you think independence can ever be achieved without violence, protest, and bloodshed? Explain your answer.

2. Indira served as her father's hostess and often went with him on his trips throughout the world. In what way did this prepare her for her role as prime minister?

3. Why do you think the Congress party considered Indira as the person to take her father's place?

4. What additional skills did Indira gain that made her feel more qualified to be prime minister in 1966 than in 1964?

5. In 1975, when some people thought she should resign, Indira instead put her opponents in jail. Why do you think she did this? What does this tell you about the kind of woman Indira was?

6. Despite her problems with the Sikhs, Indira used Sikh bodyguards. Why do you think she did this? What does this tell you about the kind of woman Indira was?

7. Why do you think people questioned whether Indira would be able to lead India?

8. India is a country with many problems. Why do you think these problems would make it a difficult country to govern? In your opinion, what kind of leader would India need in order to manage some of its problems?

QUOTABLE QUOTES

Indira Gandhi once said, "I don't mind if my life goes in the service of the nation. If I die, every drop of my blood will invigorate the nation." What do you think this statement means? Do you agree or disagree with this statement? Explain.

ACTIVITIES

1. As prime minister, Indira often met with leaders of other lands, including the president of the United States. Imagine that you are Indira Gandhi. You have just arrived in the United States and are prepared to hold discussions with the president. What will you talk about?

You will want to prepare an agenda, a list of topics you will discuss. You might want to talk about some of the problems India faces. You may want the United States to give money to help India. You may want to discuss problems that concern both countries. What else will you include in your agenda?

With a partner, decide who will act out the part of Indira and who will be the president. Then hold your meeting. As you prepare for your meeting, think about these things: Who will speak first? Will your meeting be friendly or will you argue over some points on your agenda? How will you end your meeting?

From *Notable Women*, by Arlene J. Morris-Lipsman, Copyright © 1990 Scott, Foresman and Company.

2. When Indira was born, a well-known Indian poet wrote a poem describing her. Imagine now that the year is 1984 and that Indira has just been killed. You are a famous Indian poet, and you have decided to write a poem in memory of your slain leader.

Write a poem of at least four lines. You may want to write about one of these four topics: Indira's character, her contributions, how you felt about her, or her death. Remember, it is not always necessary for a poem to rhyme.

When everyone has finished their poems, read them aloud to your classmates. Then display them on the bulletin board or around the room.

FOR FURTHER RESEARCH

1. Indira is the third generation of Nehrus to lead India. Her father and grandfather were also important political figures. Find out more about Indira's grandfather, Motilal Nehru, and her father, Jawaharlal Nehru, and their accomplishments. What did Indira learn from these two men?

2. Find out more about how Indira Gandhi worked to solve some of India's problems when she was prime minister of that country. What programs did she establish to help the many poor people? Did she set up any educational programs to end illiteracy in her nation? What else did she do to help her people?

3. Find out more about the Sikhs, who wanted independence from India. Did Indian leaders learn anything from Indira's assassination? Were the Sikhs given their independence? Why do you think Indira Gandhi refused to listen to the Sikh demands? Do you feel the Sikhs should have been given their independence? Why?

FOR FURTHER READING

Garnett, Emmeline. *Madame Prime Minister: The Story of Indira Gandhi.* New York: Farrar, Straus & Giroux, 1967.

Greene Carol. *Indira Nehru Gandhi: Ruler of India.* Chicago: Children's Press, 1985.

Lamb, Beatrice Pitney. *The Nehrus of India: Three Generations of Leadership.* New York: Macmillan, 1967.

Margaret Thatcher

Prime Minister
1925–

MARGARET THATCHER WAS ONCE CALLED "the Iron Lady." How did the Iron Lady prove herself to the world?

By the time she was ten, Margaret Roberts was already involved in politics. On election day, she busied herself by running errands for England's Conservative party. As young as she was, Margaret supported the Conservatives, just like her father.

But in 1935, what really mattered to Margaret was school. A good student in elementary school, Margaret longed to go to the university when she got older.

At last, when she was seventeen, Margaret enrolled in Oxford University. Of course she spent much of her time studying (chemistry), but once again she was involved in politics. She had joined the Oxford University Conservative Association and eventually became the group's first woman president. Only twenty-one, she secretly thought that one day she might like to serve in Parliament. (Parliament makes the laws that govern Great Britain.) For now, though, upon graduation, she would work as a chemist.

As time went by, Margaret often thought about politics. At last she decided to include her name among the list of Conservative candidates in the 1950 election who hoped to represent the district of Dartford. Party leaders would choose one from among the twenty-three names, and the person chosen would then run for a seat in Parliament.

How Margaret hoped she would be chosen—and she was! Despite her best efforts, Margaret lost the election to the Labour party candidate. However, the following year she was nominated once more as the Conservative candidate. Once again, she failed to win a seat in Parliament.

By now Margaret had married Denis Thatcher, and in 1953 she became the proud mother of twins. Still concerned about her career, however, Margaret had begun to study law. Passing her bar exam, she became a tax lawyer.

Politics, though, was never far from her mind. For a while Conservative party leaders felt she belonged at home with her children. But finally, in 1959, Margaret was nominated as the Conservative candidate from the Finchley district. Enthusiastically, she urged the people of Finchley to vote for her. When the ballots were finally counted, Margaret Thatcher had won the election. At last, she was a Member of Parliament (M.P.).

As an M.P., Margaret began to earn a reputation as a hard worker and as a valuable member of the party. Slowly her power increased, and more and more, she was given important assignments. During all these years, however, the Labour party, not the Conservatives, actually headed the British government. In the 1970 election, though, the Conservatives were declared the winners. Now it was their turn to run the government. As for Margaret, she was invited to become the secretary of education in the new government. Eagerly she accepted the position.

Now in charge of her country's educational system, Margaret worked to develop teacher training programs and pushed for school construction. Wanting to improve Britain's schools, she traveled frequently, studying school systems throughout the world.

For four years, Margaret Thatcher served in the government, but in 1974, the Conservatives lost the election. Now trouble arose in the party. Many Conservative M.P.'s were dissatisfied with their party leader, Edward Heath. Desperately they looked among themselves for a new leader. In 1975 they chose Margaret Thatcher to become the leader of their party. If the Conservatives won the next election, Margaret would become Britain's next prime minister. And on May 4, 1979, that's exactly what happened.

Many Britons questioned whether Margaret could do the job, but she was not worried. The woman whom the Russians had once called "the Iron Lady" was ready to lead her country.

As prime minister, Margaret handled many problems, among them high inflation and high unemployment. She even led her country through a short war in the faraway Falkland Islands. Thrilled with their wartime victory and satisfied that Margaret was doing her job, Britons reelected her to a second term in 1983. In 1987, she began serving her third term.

During her long stay in power, Margaret made many changes. Some were popular, others were not. However, Margaret Thatcher always believed she was doing her best for Britain. She had forced open the doors to become the first woman prime minister of a major European country. She had proven to the world that a woman could indeed lead her country into the twenty-first century.

FOR DISCUSSION

1. Margaret kept her dream of becoming an M.P. a secret for a while. What do you think her family and friends would have said if she had shared her plans with them?

2. Why do you think the Russians referred to Margaret as the Iron Lady? What other nicknames would fit her? Explain your answer.

3. What qualifications do you think Margaret had in order to be chosen as the Conservative party leader?

4. Even though Margaret rose higher and higher in the Conservative party, she did not consider that she might one day be prime minister of her country. Why do you suppose she felt this way?

QUOTABLE QUOTES

Margaret Thatcher once said, "If you want anything said, ask a man; if you want anything done, ask a woman." What do these words mean to you? Can you give examples to either support or refute this quote?

ACTIVITIES

1. Collect and share newspaper and magazine articles dealing with England. Select one of the articles and use it as a basis for a comic strip.

To create your comic strip, take a large sheet of unlined paper and divide it into four equal sections. Within each section, draw a picture of Margaret Thatcher as she deals with the situation described in the article you chose. Your drawings may be lifelike or they may be comic strip characters. You may also want to include a conversation balloon to write down some of the things Margaret might have said or thought.

2. To remember all the important things she must do each day, Margaret Thatcher probably keeps a schedule. Imagine that you are Margaret. You are about to prepare your schedule of events for tomorrow. Think about what you will be doing then.

On a sheet of paper write the hours of the day in the left-hand margin, going down the page in a column. Next to each hour, write what you will be doing. What time will you arrive at work? Mark this down on your schedule. What will you do first? Perhaps you will be meeting with the president of the United States from 9:00 A.M. to 11:00 A.M. Include this meeting in your schedule. What will you do at noon? At 1:00 P.M.? When will you leave the office?

When you have finished your schedule, look it over. Of all your activities, which one do you think is the most important? On a sheet of paper, write a brief paragraph identifying your most important job and explain why it is so important. Remember, you are still Margaret Thatcher. Try to think as she would.

When you have finished your schedules and reports, share them with your classmates by reading them aloud.

From *Notable Women*, by Arlene J. Morris-Lipsman, Copyright © 1990 Scott, Foresman and Company.

FOR FURTHER RESEARCH

1. Find out more about the Conservative party Margaret Thatcher heads. What are some of its beliefs? What sorts of changes did Margaret and her Conservative party make in Britain?

2. Find out more about how England's Parliament works. Who makes up the Parliament? How are the laws actually passed? How is Parliament similar to or different from the United States Congress? What kinds of activities might Margaret have been involved in when she was in Parliament?

3. Find out more about Margaret Thatcher's foreign policies. Who are her strongest allies? On what major issues has Margaret sided with the United States? On what issues has she differed? How has she gotten along with the presidents of the United States?

FOR FURTHER READING

Faber, Doris. *Margaret Thatcher: Britain's "Iron Lady."* New York: Puffin Books, 1986.

Sandra Day O'Connor

Supreme Court Justice
1930–

SANDRA DAY O'CONNOR IS MAKING DECISIONS that affect our entire country. What events led her to the highest Court in our land?

When Sandra Day was only five years old, her parents made a decision. Their daughter was too bright to be educated at the schools that were near their ranch home in southeastern Arizona. So they sent her to live with her grandparents in El Paso, Texas. There she would attend a private girls' school and get a good education.

Sandra missed her home during those long school years. But she also knew how important a good education was. She worked hard at her studies and did so well that she was able to graduate from high school when she was only sixteen.

At this time, in the late 1940s, high school often meant the end of education for many girls. But not for Sandra. She decided to go on to college, to Stanford University in California.

As usual, Sandra did well in school. Unlike most of her female classmates who were preparing to be teachers, Sandra had decided to study economics. Then a class in business law interested her so much that she decided to become a lawyer. She knew that many law schools did not admit women, but that didn't stop her. She applied and was accepted into Stanford's law school. A few years later, in 1952, a proud Sandra had earned her law degree. She was now ready to begin work as a lawyer.

Finding a position was difficult. Sandra applied to several big law firms, but none accepted her. No one was interested in hiring a woman. Sandra eventually took a job as a law clerk with the government, which did hire women.

By this time, Sandra had met John O'Connor. In late 1952, she and John were married.

After living in Germany for a while, the O'Connors returned to live in Phoenix, Arizona. Sandra was expecting her first child. After the baby came, she wanted to devote her time to caring for him. Soon, however, Sandra felt the need to do more, so she took a part-time job as a lawyer. But when her second child was born, she decided to stay at home and raise her children. She worked as a full-time mother for five years, but she also found time to get involved in her community and in politics.

At last, when Sandra was thirty-five, she knew it was time to resume her career. She applied to become an assistant attorney general for the State of Arizona, and she was hired. Sandra worked hard and earned a good reputation as a lawyer.

In 1969 Sandra made an important career decision. She ran for office and became an Arizona state senator. Now she would have the chance to help make the laws for her state. In her new position, she thought about some of the laws that were unfair to women, and she worked to change them. Even though she was very busy, she still found time to be with her family. They were important to her.

After five years, Sandra made another career change. She was elected to the post of superior court judge in 1974. Then, in 1979, the governor of Arizona appointed her to be judge in the state court of appeals. As a judge, Sandra was tough but fair, and she was respected. Sandra was very happy now. She had a job she loved. She had her family, and she was active in her community. But things were about to change for Sandra Day O'Connor.

In 1979, Ronald Reagan had been elected president of the United States. He had promised the people that he would appoint a woman to the Supreme Court. The Supreme Court is the highest Court in the country, and it decides on cases that are important to the nation.

One late, hot July afternoon, Sandra got a call from President Reagan. He asked her if she would like to be a judge on the Supreme Court. Of course, Sandra said yes.

Now it was up to the United States Senate. They would have to decide if she would make a good judge. Their decision was yes, she would.

And so, in September 1981 Sandra Day O'Connor became the first woman ever to sit on the Supreme Court. It was a great honor for her and for women throughout the country.

Sandra's desire to succeed and her hard work had paid off. With great dignity Sandra put on her black judge's robe. She knew that for the rest of her working life she would proudly serve her country.

FOR DISCUSSION

1. When Sandra attended school in the 1940s, high school was often the end of a girl's education. Why weren't girls encouraged to continue their education?

2. Even though Sandra knew that many law schools did not admit women, she decided to apply anyway. What qualities did Sandra possess that enabled her to do this? Share an experience in which you showed similar qualities.

3. When Sandra couldn't get a job with a big law firm, she took the job as a law clerk with the government. How do you think she felt about this decision?

4. Although Sandra Day O'Connor occupies a very high position, she has lived her life like many other women. She has faced some of the problems that many other women have faced. Identify some of these problems.

5. Sandra changed careers many times in her life. She was a lawyer, a state senator, and then a judge. How do you think all these career changes prepared Sandra to hold the position of Supreme Court justice?

6. What training and qualities are most important for a judge to possess? List these qualities and then put a 1 by the quality you feel is most important, a 2 by the next most important and so on. Be ready to defend your choices.

7. Why do you think President Reagan promised the people that he would appoint a woman to the Supreme Court?

8. Why was Sandra Day O'Connor's appointment a great honor for women throughout the country? Do you think it is important for a woman to sit on the Supreme Court?

QUOTABLE QUOTES

When Sandra Day O'Connor became a senate leader for the state of Arizona, she said, "I think my job as a legislative leader will be no different because I am a woman than it would be if I were a man." Later, when she was asked how she wanted to be remembered in history, Sandra said, "The tombstone question—what do I want on the tombstone? I hope it might say, 'Here lies a good judge.'" What do these comments tell you about Sandra? Which do you think is more important to her, being the first woman to hold a position or doing the best she can in that position? Defend your answer.

ACTIVITIES

1. Sandra Day O'Connor and the eight other justices who make up the Supreme Court listen to many kinds of cases, including discrimination cases. In the United States, it is against the law to discriminate—to take away a person's rights or freedoms because of his or her race, religion, or gender.

Read the following story. Then follow the directions for holding a trial about the case.

> Each year eight students were invited to join Homer School's Helping Hands Club. Meeting weekly, club members would make toys for the children in the city's hospitals.

In order to belong to the club, a student had to have good grades and be recognized as a school leader. Since the club had been organized, its members had always been girls, and it was considered a girls' club.

This year, nine students applied to join the club. One of them, Eric, was a boy. He was an A student and president of his class. He was involved in several other school clubs. He had all the qualifications necessary to join the Helping Hands Club. When the final selections were made, however, Eric was not invited to join.

Eric believed that he was refused membership because he was a boy.

Imagine that Eric decided to challenge the club's decision in court and that the case is now being heard before the Supreme Court. Imagine that your classroom is the Supreme Court. Conduct a trial for this case in your classroom. You will need to act out roles for the following: nine Supreme Court justices, lawyers representing both Eric and the Helping Hands Club, Eric, and members of the club.

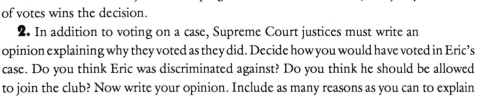

It will be necessary for the trial lawyers to prepare arguments: to explain why their clients feel as they do and why Eric should or should not be admitted to the club. These arguments should be presented before a panel of Supreme Court justices who will make the final decision. Was Eric discriminated against? Should he be allowed to join the Helping Hands Club? Remember, a majority of votes wins the decision.

2. In addition to voting on a case, Supreme Court justices must write an opinion explaining why they voted as they did. Decide how you would have voted in Eric's case. Do you think Eric was discriminated against? Do you think he should be allowed to join the club? Now write your opinion. Include as many reasons as you can to explain your decision.

FOR FURTHER RESEARCH

1. Find out more about the Supreme Court. Who are some of the other justices who make up the Supreme Court? How long have they served? Which president appointed them?

2. Find out how a case actually gets to be heard before the Supreme Court. What kinds of cases are heard before the Court?

3. Research one of the cases heard by the Supreme Court during the time Sandra Day O'Connor has been a Supreme Court justice. Describe the case, the ruling, and how Sandra Day O'Connor voted. What lasting effect will the case have on our country? Compare your findings with those of your classmates and compare Sandra Day O'Connor's stands on the issues with those of the other Supreme Court justices. What similarities or differences can you find?

FOR FURTHER READING

Bentley, Judith. *Justice Sandra Day O'Connor*. New York: Julian Messner, 1983.

Greene, Carol. *Sandra Day O'Connor: First Woman on the Supreme Court*. Chicago: Children's Press, 1982.

Benazir Bhutto

Prime Minister
1953–

S A YOUNGSTER IN ISLAMIC PAKISTAN, Benazir Bhutto learned early that women were not expected to do much more than marry and raise children. Yet, as she grew older, she came to want more out of life. Eventually she achieved what no other Moslem woman had. What did Benazir do?

Sixteen-year-old Benazir Bhutto walked slowly, stopping often to take in the strange sights and sounds that surrounded her. How different her life was here in the United States, she thought. Back home in Pakistan she had been the pampered daughter of Zulfikar Ali Bhutto, a wealthy landowner. Here at Radcliffe College, there was no one who would spoil her. Well, she decided, she would just have to get used to it.

Determined to adjust to her new life, Benazir tucked her shalwar khameez (long tops over loose pants) into the closet and replaced them with American jeans and sweatshirts. Soon she became involved in popular American student causes as well.

Marching in protest against the Vietnam War was one of her political activities. But it was the women's movement that fascinated her most. True, unlike most Pakistani women, she had been encouraged by her father to study. But now she was discovering that women did not have to sit quietly by and do as they were told. No, they could choose their own destinies.

News from home caused Benazir to protest again, this time alone and in defense of her own country. Pakistan was involved in an unpopular war with neighboring India. Although she was saddened to learn of her country's surrender, she was thrilled to learn that her beloved father had become Pakistan's president, then its prime minister.

Inspired by her father, Benazir graduated from Radcliffe with a degree in government in 1973. Then it was on to England—Oxford University—where she continued her studies in philosophy, economics, and of course, politics.

Returning to Pakistan in 1977, she planned a career in government—foreign service. But her dreams were quickly shattered when a few days after her return, her father's government was overthrown and he was imprisoned and charged with murder.

Of course, Benazir protested—so much that she, too, was eventually jailed. In and out of prison several times between 1977 and 1979, she was powerless to help her father. In 1979 he was executed.

Angry now, Benazir, who had become recognized as the leader of her father's party, had made up her mind. The man who had had her father killed, General Mohammed Zia-ul-Haq, Pakistan's prime minister, must be removed from power.

All too soon, however, Benazir discovered how difficult this mission could be. Gathering large crowds around her to protest against the government, demanding free elections (Prime Minister Zia would not allow them), she was thrown in jail, in 1979 and again in 1981. For three years she remained in prison, suffering through the winter cold, sweltering in the 120-degree summer heat, battling the swarms of insects that buzzed around her. Finally, in 1984, Benazir was released. Thin and sick, she left Pakistan for England to seek medical help.

Putting the past behind her, Benazir returned to Pakistan in 1986. Delighting the huge crowds that welcomed her back, Benazir promised that she would continue her fight against Zia's government. For those who asked about her personal life, she answered that marriage was not in her future plans. No, her country came first.

In 1987, however, Benazir shocked everyone, perhaps even herself, when she agreed to a marriage arranged by her family. Believing that a woman could have both a marriage and a career, Benazir wed Asif Zardari in 1987.

Marriage and even the birth of her son could not stop Benazir Bhutto. When, following General Zia's death in a plane crash, the government announced that free elections to choose a prime minister would indeed be held, Benazir was ready. In November 1988, she led her party to victory. A few weeks later, on December 2, 1988, Benazir was sworn in as the first woman prime minister of a Moslem nation.

The road she had taken would not be an easy one, she knew. Many people in and out of Pakistan questioned whether she would be able to lead her country. Why, she had never even held a salaried job, they said. And more, Pakistan had so many problems—poverty and ethnic tensions, for instance. Could Benazir, a woman, really do the job? But she was not afraid. Ready to serve her country, Benazir Bhutto looked eagerly toward the future.

FOR DISCUSSION

1. Why do you think Benazir was sent to a college in the United States instead of being sent to one in Pakistan?

2. Benazir Bhutto was raised in a society that didn't expect much of women. Do you think Benazir felt any conflicts between what the women's movement was teaching her and her own upbringing? Explain your answer.

3. At first Benazir planned a career in foreign service. It wasn't until after her father's death that she considered a career in politics. Why do you think she chose foreign service over politics?

4. In a Moslem nation, women usually hold little power. Why do you think her party chose Benazir as its leader instead of a man?

5. Why do you think Prime Minister Zia feared Benazir and had her arrested so often?

6. In an arranged marriage, a woman has no say in choosing her husband. Benazir was an educated woman with a mind of her own. Why do you think she agreed to an arranged marriage?

QUOTABLE QUOTES

Benazir once told a crowd of her supporters, "He [her father] told me at our last meeting at the Rawalpindi jail that I must sacrifice everything for my country. This is a mission I shall live or die for." In what way has Benazir already proven these words to be true?

ACTIVITIES

1. Before she became prime minister, Benazir Bhutto took every opportunity she had to speak about her plans to make Pakistan a better country.

Imagine that the year is 1986 and you are Benazir Bhutto. A reporter from a United States television network has asked you to talk to him and to the American people. You will be seen live on tonight's 6:00 news for a four-minute interview. What will you tell this reporter and the people of America? Prepare a brief script and include what you wish to tell the American people about what is happening in your country, about your goals for Pakistan. Remember, you will be on the air for only four minutes, so you must include only the most important information.

When you have finished writing your remarks, share them with your classmates. Choose a student to act as the reporter. He or she will introduce you to the television audience. The reporter will then ask you to tell the audience about conditions in Pakistan. As you speak, try to imagine how Benazir would say the words.

Your interviewer may also ask you a few questions when you have finished. Try to answer them as you think Benazir would.

2. During her lifetime, and before she became prime minister, Benazir participated in a number of protest rallies against the Zia government. During protest rallies, demonstrators often sing songs to keep up their spirits or to show they are united. Perhaps Benazir Bhutto led her people in song.

Working in a small group, imagine that the year is 1986 and that you are about to participate in a Pakistani protest rally. During your rally, you will be singing a song that represents your thoughts and feelings.

Write a song that you might sing as you gather together to protest Zia's government. Choose a melody that you are familiar with, perhaps a song you sing in school, or perhaps you might choose the American protest song "We Shall Overcome." Think about the melody of that song. Now write your own words to fit that melody. Your words should describe how you think and feel.

When each group has finished its song, sing them for each other.

FOR FURTHER RESEARCH

1. Locate Pakistan on your world map or globe. Now find out more about Pakistan's history. What has its relationship been with neighboring India? What people live in Pakistan? What are some problems Pakistan has experienced?

2. Benazir Bhutto adored her father. Find out more about Zulfikar Ali Bhutto. What kind of leader was he? How did he influence is daughter?

3. Find out more about Pakistan's relationship with the United States. Find out how Benazir Bhutto feels about the United States. What kind of relationship do you think she will have with our country?

FOR FURTHER READING

(No books in print as of now.)

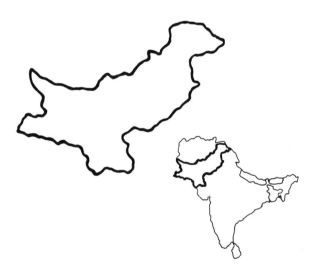

THINKING IT OVER

1. How have these five women affected the roles of women today in government and law? Explain.

2. Which woman do you think has made the greatest contribution to increasing the leadership roles of women? Why? In your opinion, which of the five women had greater obstacles to overcome? Explain.

3. Do you think these five women caused a change in women's roles, or do you think they were "at the right place at the right time" when the roles of women were beginning to change? Explain.

4. What conditions existed in their countries that made it possible for Margaret Thatcher to become prime minister of Great Britain, Indira Gandhi to become prime minister of India, Golda Meir to become prime minister of Israel, Benazir Bhutto to become prime minister of Pakistan, and Sandra Day O'Connor to become a Supreme Court justice? What similarities can you find? What differences can you find?

5. Golda Meir, Indira Gandhi, Benazir Bhutto, and Margaret Thatcher represent the handful of women who have been chosen to lead their countries. Why do you think so few countries have chosen women to serve as their leaders?

6. Among the four female prime ministers—Golda Meir, Indira Gandhi, Benair Bhutto, and Margaret Thatcher—which woman do you think was more readily accepted by her people to be a candidate for prime minister? Why do you think this was so?

7. Which of the four prime ministers do you think had the most difficult time trying to make a career for herself in politics? Why do you think this was so?

8. Compare the life experiences of Indira Gandhi and Benazir Bhutto. In what ways were their lives similar? What lessons can Benazir Bhutto learn from Indira Gandhi?

SCIENCE

Maria Mitchell

Astronomer
1818–1889

O N OCTOBER 6, 1848 MARIA MITCHELL, an American, received a gold medal from the king of Denmark for her work in astronomy. What did Maria do to earn her medal?

Twelve-year-old Maria Mitchell ran eagerly to her father's side. In just a few minutes, the eclipse of the sun began. Not only did Maria watch the eclipse through her father's telescope (through smoked glass to protect her eyes), she also helped him record his observations.

How excited Maria was! The sky was fascinating, she thought. Night after night, she peered through the telescope, studying the heavens. Already she was becoming a skilled astronomer and her father's best assistant.

Scanning the heavens above her home on the island of Nantucket, Massachusetts was not enough for Maria, however. As she grew older, she poured through thick volumes of books on astronomy, navigation, and mathematics. Slowly, with her father's help, she educated herself.

How thrilled she was in 1836 when she began to work as a librarian for the Nantucket library. Now she could spend endless hours reading the great scientific books that lined the shelves.

Busy during the day, she was even busier at night. Her father had been hired to make observations of the stars for the government. Maria worked along side of him, helping him.

One October evening in 1847, Maria returned home from the library. Eagerly she rushed up to the roof of her house and took her place at the telescope. Slowly she began to sweep the skies. Suddenly she stopped. She had noticed a tiny white speck in the sky. Maria had never seen it before. What could it be, she wondered?

Quickly she called her father. Checking her observations, Mr. Mitchell turned to his daughter. She had discovered a comet, he told her proudly.

Immediately he reported Maria's discovery to the proper scientific authorities. They soon agreed. Maria Mitchell had indeed discovered a comet.

As the first discoverer of a telescopic comet, Maria was now eligible to receive a gold medal offered by the king of Denmark. But was she really the first to discover the comet? An astronomer in Rome had also reported sighting it. A great debate raged through the world's scientific community. At last a decision was reached. Maria Mitchell was awarded the gold medal, and the comet was named in her honor.

By now Maria had become famous, especially in the scientific world. More and more she was asked to work on major astronomical projects. She also became the first woman to be invited to join several important scientific societies. And when Maria traveled through Europe in 1857, leading scientists throughout the world were delighted to meet her.

Shortly after Maria returned from Europe, her mother died. Now she and her father moved to Lynn, Massachusetts where they continued to study the sky.

One day in 1862 Maria Mitchell received a visitor, a representative of Matthew Vassar. Mr. Vassar, Maria learned, had decided to open a college for women. Concerned that women should study science, he planned to build an observatory and furnish it with the finest equipment. More important, Mr. Vassar wanted Maria Mitchell to become the school's professor of astronomy.

How could she teach college students, Maria wondered, when she had never been to college? But Mr. Vassar knew Maria could do the job. She had an excellent reputation as a scientist.

Promising to think about the offer, she at last accepted it, and in September 1865 Maria Mitchell took on her first group of students. For over twenty years, Maria enthusiastically taught students all she knew about astronomy.

Maria busied herself in other ways, too. She became the first astronomer to photograph the sun's surface, and she carefully studied the planets Jupiter and Saturn.

Even more, she had been elected the president of the Syracuse Congress of the Association for the Advancement of Women. Now she talked about the need for women in science, for women to be educated, for women's equal rights.

Maria Mitchell finally retired from her teaching position in 1888. A year later, she quietly passed away.

She had spent a lifetime observing the sky and sharing her knowledge with all who cared to learn. Her childhood home in Nantucket became a museum, the Maria Mitchell Museum, in her honor. It is a lasting memory to this great woman of science, America's first woman astronomer.

FOR DISCUSSION

1. Do you think it is important for scientists to study and observe the skies? Explain your answer.

2. Why do you think it was necessary for Maria to educate herself?

3. In 1836 Maria began to work in the Nantucket library, even though she was already a skilled astronomer. Why do you think Maria worked as a librarian instead of as an astronomer?

4. When Vassar first opened its doors, many people questioned whether such a college for women should exist. Why do you think so many people were against the idea of having a women's college?

5. Even though Vassar was a girls' school, few women were chosen to teach there. Why do you think Mr. Vassar asked Maria to be professor of astronomy instead of choosing a male scientist?

6. Why do you think Maria became involved with the Syracuse Congress of the Association for the Advancement of Women?

QUOTABLE QUOTES

Maria Mitchell once said, "A sphere is not made up of one, but of an infinite number of circles; women have diverse gifts and to say that women's sphere is the family circle is a mathematical absurdity." What do these words mean to you? What other circles might Maria say make up a woman's "sphere"?

ACTIVITIES

1. Maria Mitchell kept a diary in which she recorded her thoughts and feelings.

Imagine now that the year is 1847 and that you are Maria Mitchell. You have just discovered a comet, and you are being considered to receive a gold medal for your discovery. However, the scientific community is debating whether you were the first one to sight the comet.

Write a diary entry explaining your thoughts and feelings on this matter. Do you want to receive the medal? Is it important to you? Why? How do you feel, knowing that scientists throughout the world are talking about you? How do you think your beloved father feels about all of this? What else will you include in your diary? Be sure to date your diary entry before you begin to write.

When you have finished your diary entries, share them with each other by reading them aloud.

2. As a professor at Vassar, Maria may have talked to both parents and students about the role education played in a young girl's life.

Imagine now that one of Maria's students, along with her father, has come to talk to her. The father wants his daughter to drop out of school after only one year in college. The daughter, of course, is unhappy with her father's decision.

In your classroom, act out this situation. Divide into groups of three, and choose who will be Maria, the father, and the daughter. Before you play this scene, think about how your character feels and what he or she might say about this matter. If you have been selected to play the part of Maria, think carefully about what you will tell the father. How do you think Maria Mitchell felt about educating young women?

Now, without rehearsing it beforehand, present your scene to your classmates. (Maria would not have had a chance to practice her speech.) Decide who will speak first. Think about how you will end your conversation.

FOR FURTHER RESEARCH

1. Find out more about comets. What exactly are they? Can you name any comets? Do you know who discovered them?

2. One of Maria's earliest scientific projects was observing an eclipse. Find out more about eclipses. What happens during an eclipse? How often do eclipses occur? What is the difference between a lunar eclipse and a solar eclipse?

3. Find out more about today's Vassar College. Is it still an all-female school? What kinds of subjects are taught at Vassar? How does Vassar rate among today's colleges?

FOR FURTHER READING

Baker, Rachel, and Joanna Baker Merlen. *America's First Woman Astronomer: Maria Mitchell.* New York: Julian Messner, 1960.

Wilkie, Katharine. *Maria Mitchell.* Champaign, Ill.: Garrard Publishing Company, 1966.

SCIENCE

Marie Curie

Physicist
1867–1934

MARIE CURIE UNLOCKED THE DOOR to one of science's many mysteries. Her discovery changed the way scientists viewed the world. What did Marie Curie discover?

Sixteen-year-old Manya Sklodovska rose proudly when her name was announced. She had just received the gold medal for achievement in high school. But the award had really come as no surprise to anyone. Manya had always been an excellent student.

Now that she had graduated from high school, Manya wondered what she would do with her life. Nothing interested her more than physics and chemistry, but she could not study at the University in Warsaw, Poland, her hometown. Women were not accepted as students there. But a school called the Sorbonne in Paris did accept women, and Manya's dream was to study there.

Because she did not have enough money to attend college, she worked as a governess for several years. Finally, in 1891, twenty-three year old Manya's dream came true. At long last she was on her way to Paris.

Manya, the student, was now known by her new French name, Marie. Marie knew that her classmates were curious about her. Not many women studied physics and chemistry. But that didn't bother her. Nor did she worry that she had very little money to live on. She was too happy studying to care about anything else.

For two years Marie studied hard, so hard that sometimes she even forgot to eat. Then in 1893 she was ready to take her test. She not only passed but was the first in her class. She now had a masters degree in physics. A year later she received her second degree, in mathematics.

A short time later, while Marie was working on a special research project, she met the famous scientist Pierre Curie. They fell in love and were married in 1895.

Although she worked hard at being a good wife and now a mother, Marie also continued with her scientific research. One day she read something that fascinated her. Certain natural substances (they were called elements) gave off their own invisible rays. Marie wanted to learn all she could about this radioactivity, as she called it.

Working with Pierre in a damp, unheated office that she used as a laboratory, Marie experimented with all the known natural elements. Soon she came to a startling conclusion. She felt she had discovered another radioactive element, one other scientists knew nothing about.

Of course, Marie had to prove that this element existed before her idea would be accepted. For four years the Curies worked hard, their laboratory an old, abandoned shack. Then one great day in 1902, they achieved success. Proudly, Marie introduced her new element, radium, to the scientific world.

But her work was not done. As she continued to learn about radium, she made many exciting discoveries. She even learned that radium could be used to help people who were suffering from cancer.

By this time, Marie and her husband had become famous. They received many awards and honors, including the Nobel Prize in physics in 1903.

The Curies were busy, but very happy. Then suddenly, in 1906, tragedy struck. Pierre was killed in an accident. Grief stricken, Marie wondered how she would ever get along without him. But she knew that she must continue with her work. Pierre would have wanted that.

So she continued alone, and in 1922 she received her second Nobel Prize, this time in chemistry, for her work with radium. This was the first time anyone had won two Nobel Prizes.

Marie became the director of a fine new laboratory in Paris, the Radium Institute. In all her years as a scientist, this was her first real laboratory. She was busier than ever, but she still found time to come to America, where she received many awards and honors.

As the years passed, Marie often felt tired and sick. One day in May 1934, she became very ill. A few months later, she died. Her death had been caused by too much exposure to radium.

Marie had dedicated her life to science. Now the scientific world, as well as people everywhere, mourned her death. She had been a gifted woman, a great scientist.

From *Notable Women*, by Arlene J. Morris-Lipsman, Copyright © 1990 Scott, Foresman and Company.

FOR DISCUSSION

1. As a governess, Marie cared for a family's children and tutored them. Given what you know about Marie Curie, do you think this type of work satisfied her? Explain why you answered as you did.

2. In the late 1890s, many women were satisfied just being a wife and mother. But Marie Curie continued to do scientific research despite her family roles. Why do you think she continued to study? What does this tell you about the kind of woman she was?

3. Marie made her great discovery in an old, abandoned shack. For years, she and Pierre had begged his school for a real laboratory, but they had not been given one. Why do you think the school denied their request?

4. If Marie Curie had been living today, it might have been easier for her to do her work. What advantages do today's scientists have that Marie Curie didn't have? Can you think of any advantages Marie had that today's scientists do not?

5. Marie's death was caused by an overexposure to radium. If she would have known about radium's effects earlier, do you think she would have continued her work? Explain why you answered as you did.

QUOTABLE QUOTES

Marie and her husband had discovered the way to obtain pure radium by taking it out of another substance, pitchblende. They could have patented their method, which meant they would have controlled the production of radium all over the world. They would have become rich. However, they could have also shared their findings with anyone who asked, for free. This is what they chose to do. When Marie thought about keeping the information to themselves, she said, "It is impossible. It would be contrary to the scientific spirit." What do her words mean to you? What is the scientific spirit?

ACTIVITIES

1. Imagine you are a reporter working for a major newspaper when Marie Curie made her discovery. Your editor has asked you to write a story about Marie's scientific breakthrough, her discovery of radium.

Write a newspaper article about this event. Be sure to include information that answers as many of these five questions as possible: who, when, where, what, and why. Begin your article with a good lead sentence. You want to capture your readers' attention. You may also want to include a brief background of Marie's life and information about her future plans. What other information would your readers be interested in knowing? Include it in your article. Use the biography of Marie Curie and any other additional reference material you wish to help you write your article.

When your class has finished their stories, read them aloud to each other. You may want to put all the stories together to make a book about Marie Curie. Be sure to give your book a title.

2. Imagine you are a newspaper reporter living during the time Marie Curie made her important discovery. Your editor has obtained permission for you to do a rare interview with Marie. (Marie did not really enjoy publicity.)

Prepare a list of questions that you would like to ask Marie. What are you curious to know about her? What would your readers like to know?

Now choose a student to act out the part of the interviewer and one to act as Marie Curie, and conduct the interview.

If you have been selected as the interviewer, think about how you would introduce yourself to this famous woman. How will you talk to her? How will you respond to her answers?

If you have been selected to portray Marie, try to answer the questions as you think she would have. Remember to think, speak, and act as Marie would have. You may want to read more about Marie Curie to find out how she would have answered these questions.

FOR FURTHER RESEARCH

1. Marie Curie's discovery of radium was important for many reasons. Find out more about radium. What are some uses of radium today?

2. Learn about some of the other recipients of the Nobel Prize in physics and in chemistry during the early 1900s. Were any of them women? For what kind of work did they receive the Nobel Prize? How do you think their work compares to that done by Marie Curie?

3. Find out more about the Sorbonne, a college that did admit women in the late 1800s. Why do you think the Sorbonne admitted women when so many other schools did not? Does this college still exist today?

FOR FURTHER READING

DeLeeuw, Adele. *Marie Curie: Woman of Genius*. Champaign, Ill: Gerrard Publishing Company, 1970.

Greene, Carol. *Marie Curie, Pioneer Physicist*. Chicago: Childrens Press, 1984.

McKown, Robin. *Marie Curie*. New York: G. P. Putnam's Sons, 1959.

 SCIENCE

Sylvia Earle

Marine Biologist
1935–

BECAUSE OF A DARING MISSION, never before performed by a woman, Sylvia Earle became a celebrity scientist. What did she do to earn her fame?

Snakes, frogs, and fish didn't scare young Sylvia Earle. In fact, she actually liked them. Sylvia was curious about other living things, too. She spent much of her childhood in the woods and marshes near her farm home in New Jersey learning all she could about nature.

When her family moved to Florida in 1948, Sylvia would often stroll along the beach collecting starfish and sea urchins. Marine (water) life was especially fascinating, she thought. Even though she was young, Sylvia felt that she would study plants and animals all her life if she could.

When Sylvia at last became a student at Florida State University, she chose botany—the science of plants—as the subject she would study. Although she was often the only woman in her classes, Sylvia was determined to do her best.

During the summer of 1953, Sylvia finally had the chance to study underwater plants and animals. To learn more about ocean life, Sylvia would have to dive deep into the water, wearing special breathing equipment. Although she had never worn SCUBA gear before, Sylvia Earle was not afraid. And she soon discovered how thrilling diving could be. But to her, the best part was actually seeing marine life in its own environment.

Sylvia spent the next few years completing her college work. Then, in 1964, she was chosen to participate in a real scientific dive, the International Indian Ocean Expedition. The only woman among a crew of sixty men, she was excited about the work she would be doing. As a marine biologist, she would be diving into the ocean to study fish and plants and their relationship to each other.

As the years passed, Sylvia continued to work on diving missions. Although it was always difficult for her to leave her children, she looked forward to each dive.

In time Sylvia began to earn a fine reputation as a marine biologist. She was so good that in 1970 she was asked to join the Tektite II Project. Seventeen teams of scientists were involved in this project. One was a five-woman team lead by Sylvia Earle.

Sylvia's assignment was a daring one. She and her team would be living underwater for two weeks in a special building called a habitat. Not only would they study ocean life, but their behavior in the cramped living space would be watched by other scientists.

The women were well prepared for their work, especially Sylvia. She had seventeen years of diving experience behind her. No other crew member could match this record.

Despite the remarks made by a few male scientists, Sylvia knew she had been chosen for the job because she could do it well—and she did.

During their two-week stay underwater near St. John in the Virgin Islands, she and the other women often spent six to ten hours outside their habitat studying ocean life. They observed many plants and animals, including sharks.

When the mission was finally completed, the women were treated like celebrities. Sylvia and her team were even invited to lunch at the White House and Sylvia was named woman of the year by the *Los Angeles Times*.

After her successful underwater stay, Sylvia was busier than ever. She participated in more dives, acting as chief scientist on many of them. During one of those dives, Sylvia swam with whales trying to learn about them. On another, she set a record for a deep dive in the Pacific Ocean. She also discovered sea plants that no one even knew existed.

Because she wanted to learn about marine life, Sylvia calmly faced the many dangers she met diving into the ocean. Those dangers didn't really bother her either. Instead, she thought about the opportunity she had to discover something new.

Sylvia was proud of her accomplishments, but she was even prouder knowing that by sharing her knowledge, she had helped others understand the miracles of the sea.

FOR DISCUSSION

1. Even as a child, Sylvia was curious about nature, and her parents encouraged this curiosity. Do you think her parents' attitude was shared by other parents who had daughters growing up in the 1940s? Explain your answer.

2. Given what you know about Sylvia Earle, how do you think she felt about the remarks some of the male scientists made as she prepared for the Tektite II Project? Why would she feel this way?

3. When the Tektite II Project was completed, Sylvia and the other women were treated like celebrities. However, the male scientists did not receive the same amount of attention. Why do you think this was so? Sylvia referred to this as "reverse discrimination." What do you think she meant?

4. Why was the Tektite II Project so important to scientists throughout the world? In what way would a two-week stay underwater be more effective or more beneficial to scientists than a dive of only a few hours?

5. Sylvia Earle has given much to science by studying ocean life. Why is ocean research so important to humankind?

QUOTABLE QUOTES

Even though it was difficult for her to leave her children when she went on diving missions, Sylvia once said, "It never occurred to me any more than to a man that I'd stop and turn off my mind because I had children. I think that because I had a strong feeling about what I wanted to do, it enabled me to continue. I never thought of it as unusual." Do you feel that Sylvia was unusual to believe as she did or do her words make sense to you? Explain your answer.

ACTIVITIES

1. As a marine biologist, Sylvia Earle is concerned about the health of the world's great bodies of water. She fears that many plant and animal species are being eliminated from the oceans and she worries that people are causing the waters to become polluted. Throughout her career, Sylvia has lectured to hundreds of people on this subject.

Imagine that you are Sylvia Earle and that you have been invited to present a talk on the state of our waters. You must now prepare your speech. What will you tell your audience?

You may want to begin by explaining how your feel. Do you believe that marine life is endangered and that the waters are polluted? If so, you might give specific examples of how these situations have occurred. If you are aware of any endangered species, you might mention them. You may want to suggest ways that people can help protect their oceans. What else would you like to tell your audience? As you prepare your speech, remember to think about the problems and solutions as Sylvia would.

When you have completed your lecture, present it to your classmates. After you have finished speaking, invite your audience to ask questions. Think carefully and try to answer these questions as Sylvia would.

2. During her two-week underwater stay, Sylvia spent hours exploring the fascinating world of marine life. She was always amazed by what she discovered.

Think about the kinds of things Sylvia might have seen. Do you know about any plants and animals that live in the ocean? You may want to look through an encyclopedia or a book about oceans to learn more about marine life.

Now that you have painted a picture of ocean life in your mind, put your thoughts on paper. Working in small groups, create an ocean scene that Sylvia Earle may have seen during her diving mission. Draw, paint, or cut and paste using a variety of materials on a large sheet of paper. Include as many plants and fish as you can. You may portray sea creatures as they really are, or you may want to create an imaginary species, one that Sylvia may actually discover one day. You might want to show what Sylvia's habitat looked like. What else could you include in your picture?

When you have finished your ocean scenes, display them around the room. What has each group portrayed? How is each picture like yours? How is it different?

You may want to write a haiku, a Japanese poem to describe your ocean scene. Using a literature book or a book about poetry, talk about how to compose a haiku. Then write your poem. Display it alongside your picture.

FOR FURTHER RESEARCH

1. Sylvia dreamed of "slipping into the skin of a whale." That opportunity came in 1977 when she had the chance to swim with whales in order to study them. Find out more about these huge mammals. What about whales makes them so interesting to a scientist like Sylvia Earle?

2. Sylvia was very excited the first time she put on SCUBA gear. Find out more about how SCUBA gear works. How are divers able to stay underwater using SCUBA gear? What do the letters in the word SCUBA stand for?

3. Sylvia enjoyed discovering and exploring different kinds of sea life. Find out more about some other plants and animals that live in our oceans. Why can some plants and animals only be found in certain oceans?

FOR FURTHER READING

Earle, Sylvia A., and Al Giddings. *Exploring the Deep Frontier: The Adventure of Man in the Sea*. Washington, D.C.: National Geographic Society, 1980.

Gleasner, Diana. *Breakthrough: Women in Science*. New York: Walker and Company, 1983, pp. 13–32.

Haber, Louis. *Women Pioneers of Science*. New York: Harcourt Brace Jovanovich, 1979, pp. 141–154.

THINKING IT OVER

1. Nobel Prizes are awarded in many fields—literature and peace efforts, for example. Why is it especially important for prizes to be offered in physics and chemistry?

2. Marie Curie and Sylvia Earle both had the opportunity to attend college. Compare and contrast their college experiences. Which woman had the more difficult time obtaining a college education? Why do you think this was so?

3. Compare the working conditions of Marie Curie and Maria Mitchell. Which woman do you think faced more challenges as she attempted to make her great scientific discovery? Explain your answer.

4. In what ways did these three women scientists pave the way for women in science today? How have women's roles in science changed over the years?

5. Which of these three scientists do you think faced the most serious challenges in having her work accepted? Why do you think this was so?

SOCIAL CONCERNS

Susan B. Anthony

Crusader
1820–1906

THE NINETEENTH AMENDMENT HAS BEEN CALLED the Susan B. Anthony Amendment. For what cause did Susan B. Anthony spend her life fighting?

Eleven-year-old Susan Brownell Anthony was annoyed. Sally Ann, she knew, was the most knowledgeable worker in Susan's father's textile mill. But simply because Sally was a woman, Sally Ann was not permitted to be the factory foreman. It was all so unfair, thought Susan.

Thinking about her own family made her happy, since they believed that men and women were equal. Her father, in fact, insisted that his daughters be educated (a most unusual belief for the time), and when Susan was older he sent her to one of the few private girls' schools.

Like the few other women who worked in the 1840s, Susan began to teach. Sadly she discovered that she earned less than male teachers.

Despite her dissatisfaction, Susan was not really interested at first to learn that a convention for women's rights had been held in 1848. What could these women possibly accomplish, she wondered. However, by 1852 Susan B. Anthony had changed her mind. Once too often she had seen how unfairly society treated women. Now she was determined to fight for their cause.

From *Notable Women*, by Arlene J. Morris-Lipsman, Copyright © 1990 Scott, Foresman and Company.

Susan became more than just a member of the women's rights group. She became one of its strongest leaders, and she battled for laws that would make women equal members of society.

Horrified that married women in New York had to give any money they earned to their husbands, Susan traveled throughout the state seeking signatures for a petition demanding that the law be changed. Although it was almost unheard of for a woman to speak before a mixed audience, Susan addressed as many groups of listeners as she could. Finally, in 1860, the New York legislature passed the Married Women's Property Bill.

Busy as she was, Susan also became a leader in the antislavery movement. She organized meetings and she herself spoke out against slavery. Often she faced crowds that booed her and even threw eggs at her.

The end of the Civil War meant freedom for the slaves. But for Susan B. Anthony, the battle was not over. Ex-slaves, she thought must be given the right to vote. Just as important, women, too, must be given that same right.

As she had done before, Susan addressed the crowds and urged them to sign her petitions. Much to her dismay, however, when the Fifteenth Amendment to the United States Constitution was passed, only black males were given the right to vote. Determined to continue her fight for women's suffrage (voting rights), Susan became a target for people who made fun of her and insulted her.

When she and another women's leader began to publish a newspaper, the *Revolution*, the verbal attacks became even stronger. Much of the public, even other women, were not ready to read about equal rights for women.

Speaking and writing, however, were simply not enough for Susan. She decided it was time to take drastic action. On November 5, 1872 she marched to the polls and cast a ballot. Two weeks later, she was arrested. Her crime, said the U.S. marshal, was that she had voted illegally. Following an unfair trial, Susan was found guilty and fined a hundred dollars. Bravely, she refused to pay the fine.

By now, however, because of the unfair trial, much of the public was on her side. She had not managed to convince a majority of people that women should vote, but she was being praised instead of criticized.

Despite her fame, Susan knew she still had a job to do. Her work would never be done until women could vote. She continued to travel and speak. She even helped organize a conference attended by women throughout the world. And, inspiring younger followers in the women's movement, Susan served for a time as president of the newly formed National American Women Suffrage Association. Never stopping for even a moment, Susan B. Anthony crusaded for a woman's right to vote until she died in 1906.

Even from her childhood, she had believed in the dignity of women, and she had spent over half a century fighting for their rights. When a constitutional amendment was finally passed in 1920 giving women the right to vote, people throughout the country paid Susan one last tribute. Officially it was called the Nineteenth Amendment. But to her dedicated followers it is known as the "Susan B. Anthony Amendment."

FOR DISCUSSION

1. Why do you think Susan was not interested at first in hearing about the 1848 women's rights convention?

2. In the 1850s few women spoke before a mixed audience of men and women. Why do you think women were not expected to talk before an audience? Why do you think Susan dared to address the crowds?

3. Why do you think people made fun of and insulted Susan? If you had met any of these people, what would you have said to them?

4. Why do you think Susan was found guilty during her trial?

5. How might history have been changed if Susan had been found "not guilty"?

6. Why do you think it took so long for women to get the right to vote?

7. Do you think it is important for women who live in a democracy to vote? Explain your answer.

QUOTABLE QUOTES

At a women's convention held in 1906, one of the speakers said this about Susan B. Anthony. "To you, Miss Anthony, belongs by right, as to no other woman in the world's history, the love and gratitude of all women in every country of the civilized globe. We, your daughters of the spirit, rise up today and call you blessed. . . ." Why do you think these words were said about Susan? Do you agree that Susan deserved the love and gratitude of women everywhere? Explain your answer.

ACTIVITIES

1. Sometimes students learn about historical heroes through educational comic books. Create your own educational comic book about the life of Susan B. Anthony.

Think about the events in Susan's life that you found most interesting. Now take a sheet of unlined paper and divide it into sections (panels). You may have two, three, or four panels to a page. Using pencil, crayons, or colored pencils, draw a picture in each panel that shows an important moment in Susan's life. Be sure to add conversation balloons and include some words so that your readers will know what your characters are saying or thinking. You may include as many pages as you wish in your comic book. Remember to add a front cover to your pages and illustrate it, too. Now staple your comic book together.

When you have finished, share your comic book with your classmates.

2. During her lifetime, Susan B. Anthony both organized and attended many women's rights conventions. As she addressed her audience, which included both women and men, Susan spoke out for a woman's right to vote as well as for other equal rights for women. Some of her listeners agreed with her. Others did not.

Imagine now that the year is 1868 and that you are attending a women's rights convention. Like all other delegates, you will have a chance to address the audience. What will you say? Will you demand that women be given the right to vote? Do you feel other equal rights are just as important? Do you feel that women already have enough rights? Why do you feel as you do?

Now prepare a speech that you will deliver to the delegates of this convention.

When everyone has finished writing and practicing his or her speeches, the class should choose a student to be in charge of the convention. This student will explain the purpose of the convention and introduce the speakers.

When you are called upon to speak, try to deliver your speech with as much feeling as you can, just as Susan would have.

As you listen to your classmates, be sure to applaud if you agree with them.

After everyone has spoken, the convention leader will close the meeting and thank you for attending.

FOR FURTHER RESEARCH

1. Susan B. Anthony was one of the early leaders of the early women's rights movement. Find out more about another early women's rights leader, Susan's friend Elizabeth Cady Stanton. How were her goals like Susan's? How were they different?

2. Find out more about the 1848 convention for women's rights. Where was this convention held? Who were some of the convention's leaders? What were some of the accomplishments of this convention?

3. Lucy Stone also fought for women's rights, just as Susan B. Anthony did. For a while Lucy and Susan had the same goals. Eventually, however, Lucy Stone broke from Susan and led her own movement. Find out more about Lucy Stone. What were her beliefs? Why did she disagree with Susan?

FOR FURTHER READING

Clinton, Susan. *The Story of Susan B. Anthony*. Chicago: Childrens Press, 1986.

Cooper, Ilene. *Susan B. Anthony*. New York: Franklin Watts, 1984.

Grant, Matthew G. *Susan B. Anthony: Crusader for Women's Rights*. Mankato, Minn.: Creative Education, 1974.

Noble, Iris. *Susan B. Anthony*. New York: Julian Messner, 1975.

Harriet Tubman

Freedom Fighter
1820?–1913

HARRIET TUBMAN WAS CALLED THE MOSES OF HER PEOPLE. What did Harriet do to earn this name?

By the time she was six, Harriet Ross understood what it meant to be a slave in Maryland. As a "hired out" slave, Harriet worked for a woman who had purchased her services from Harriet's owner.

Harriet hated the work—housework—and she dreaded the frequent whippings. But even worse was the fear that she would be sold. For in the South, where slavery existed, slaves could be sold like pieces of property. Then, Harriet knew, she would be separated forever from the parents and family she loved.

Eventually, Harriet was returned to her owner, and she began to work in the fields. One day, when she was a teenager, Harriet saw another slave leave the fields without permission. He was headed for a nearby country store. Angrily his master (overseer) followed him, hoping to catch him. Curious, Harriet followed them both.

Inside the store, the overseer ordered Harriet to help him tie the slave down, but Harriet did not move. Grabbing a heavy weight, the overseer threw it. It missed the slave and hit Harriet in the head instead. For days she was close to death. Finally, she recovered. But for the rest of her life, Harriet's old head injury would cause her to fall soundly asleep without warning.

Although she was still a slave, in 1844 Harriet was permitted to marry John Tubman, a free black man. She loved John, but she longed to go north where slavery did not exist. John Tubman, however, did not share Harriet's dream to go north. Painfully, Harriet made her decision. She would escape. And one night, in 1849, Harriet Tubman did just that.

Years before, she had listened as the slaves whispered excitedly about the Underground Railroad. Now Harriet learned that the Underground Railroad was a secret network of people who were eager to help runaway slaves. Hiding out in their safe houses, then traveling at night through woods and swamps, slaves managed to find their way north.

Risking her life—for if she were caught she would be returned to her owner—Harriet "rode" the Underground Railroad and finally reached the state of Pennsylvania. At long last, she was a free woman.

But for Harriet Tubman, her own freedom was not enough. Her family had to be rescued from slavery—and she would do it. Year after year, until 1860, Harriet returned to Maryland. Leading her brothers and sisters, her aged parents, and anyone else who wished to come, Harriet Tubman eventually led three hundred "passengers" on the Underground Railroad to freedom.

Her missions were filled with danger. If she were recognized or caught by a slave owner, she would be killed or severely punished. Often, Harriet disguised herself, sometimes as an old woman, sometimes as a man.

Harriet also feared for her passengers' safety. Desperately, she urged them on. Sometimes, however, a runaway would become frightened and want to turn back. Then Harriet whipped out the pistol she carried and threatened him to continue or die.

As the years passed, Harriet became famous. Black people were calling her Moses (a Bible hero who led the Jewish people out of slavery). Like Moses Harriet was leading her own people out of slavery. As for the slave owners, they began to offer rewards, often thousands of dollars, for her capture.

By this time, however, the Civil War had begun. Northern troops fought Southern ones in terrible battles. As for Harriet, she was no longer leading slaves to freedom, for they had been declared free by President Lincoln. Instead she began to work for the Northern army. Serving as a nurse, Harriet tended the sick ex-slaves. Even more, she acted as a scout and a spy for the army. With black soldiers following her, she destroyed Southern properties and freed those slaves who had not yet been released by their owners.

At last the Civil War ended, and Harriet returned to her home in Auburn, New York. Still anxious to help her people, Harriet now raised money to build schools for ex-slaves. And in 1903 she helped establish a shelter for poor, sick, and homeless blacks.

Over ninety years old, and still dedicated to her people, Harriet Tubman died on March 10, 1913.

She had served both her people and her country well. A year after she died, a bronze tablet was erected in Auburn in her memory. She will always be remembered as a remarkable woman, an American heroine.

FOR DISCUSSION

1. What conditions made it possible for slavery to exist in the South? Why do you think the Northern states did not use the system of slavery?

2. How do you think Harriet felt when she learned her husband did not share her dream of going north?

3. Although Harriet had escaped, she believed her family and others, too, must also be free, and she risked her life to help them. As a result, she was called the Moses of her people. In what ways was her life similar to and different from the life of Moses?

4. Why do you think Harriet would not let any of her passengers turn back?

5. Why do you think Harriet continued to help her people even after they were freed? What special programs would most help newly freed people? Explain your answer. Which do you think better helped her people—Harriet's leading the slaves to freedom or her schools and shelter? Explain your answer.

QUOTABLE QUOTES

Of her decision to go north, Harriet said, "I had reasoned this out in my mind; there was one of two things I had a right to, liberty or death; if I could not have one, I would have the other; for no man should take me alive, I should fight for my liberty as long as my strength lasted, and when the time came for me to go, the Lord would let them take me." What do these words mean to you? Can you think of any other Americans who also believed that the fight for liberty was worth even the risk of death? Why do you think Americans put such a high value on their right to liberty?

ACTIVITIES

1. A pantomime is a series of actions performed without words. Because they are clear, specific and well-thought out, these actions alone can tell a story.

Working in a small group, use the biography of Harriet Tubman to plan out a pantomime that will tell the story of her life. Decide who will be Harriet and who will be the other slaves. Then organize your pantomime starting with her childhood and ending with her death in 1913. You may want to make some signs that state the names of places and dates to use in your pantomime. As you practice your pantomime, make sure your actions are clear. Use your hands to make gestures, and remember that facial expressions will help your audience understand how you feel.

When you have finished planning and practicing your pantomime, present it to your classmates.

2. In your classroom, think of some of the advantages black Americans have today compared to the conditions they lived under in the 1880s. Then think about some of the disadvantages they face. List your ideas on the chalkboard.

From *Notable Women*, by Arlene J. Morris-Lipsman, Copyright © 1990 Scott, Foresman and Company.

Now imagine that Harriet Tubman is alive today and that you are Harriet. You are a very old woman with years of experience behind you.

You have decided to write a letter to an important black leader offering him or her your advice and opinions on black conditions today. What advice would you give to a black leader who is struggling to make life better for his fellow blacks? What are your opinions on current black conditions compared to those you knew in your youth?

Now write your letter. If you know the name of a black leader in this country or in your own community, address the letter to him or her.

When you have finished your letter, share it with others.

FOR FURTHER RESEARCH

1. Find out more about some of the other women living in Harriet's day who were also opposed to slavery, such as the Grimke sisters, Lucretia Mott, and Sojourner Truth. What did they do to help in the fight against slavery? How were their activities similar to Harriet Tubman's? How were they different?

2. Find out how slavery first became an accepted way of life in the United States. How did it begin? What attempts were made to end slavery in this country before the Civil War? By whom?

3. Find out more about the Underground Railroad. When and how did it begin? Who were some other people (black and white, men and women) who were connected with the Underground Railroad? Learn about some of the words used when talking about the Underground Railroad—conductor, passenger, station. What did these words mean?

FOR FURTHER READING

Brin, Ruth. *Contributions of Women: Social Reform.* Minneapolis, Minn.: Dillon Press, 1977, pp. 7–29.

Petry, Ann. *Harriet Tubman: Conductor on the Underground Railroad.* New York: Thomas Y. Crowell Company, 1955.

Sabin, Francene. *Harriet Tubman.* Mahwah, N.J.: Troll Associates, 1985.

Jane Addams

Humanitarian
1860–1935

DURING THE EARLY DAYS OF AMERICA, poor people were often feared and resented. No one even thought about helping them. During her lifetime, Jane Addams helped change America's attitude toward the poor. How did she do this?

As the carriage drove through the poor side of town, six-year-old Jane Addams looked around her curiously. Little houses crowded together, ragged children playing in trash-covered streets—her eyes took in these unhappy sights of poverty. Some day, young Jane told herself, she would own a big house and invite poor children over to play.

Even as she grew older and even after she had graduated from college in 1881, Jane still longed to help the poor. She simply did not know how to do it. And so, for many years, she spent restless, unhappy days wondering what she would do with her life.

Finally, in 1888, Jane reached a decision. She must help poor people, and now she knew how. She would establish a settlement house—the first one in America. Just as she had dreamed about long ago, she would find a big house among the rows of horrid little ones, live there herself, and open her doors to help her neighbors. And in 1889, that's exactly what Jane Addams did.

Inviting her good friend Ellen Gates Starr to join her in her plans, Jane rented a huge old house (the Hull House) in one of Chicago's poorest neighborhoods. Slowly at first, then in greater and greater numbers, her neighbors came to the Hull House. Kindly and wise, Jane soon set up programs to fit their needs.

A nursery was established, and a kindergarten. Clubs for little boys and girls and for young adults and older ones, too, were organized. Volunteers taught classes in art and music, sewing and cooking, and theater and storytelling. Jane offered practical advice to men and women working in the dark and dangerous factories nearby, and she sometimes even helped them settle their disagreements with their bosses.

As the years passed, Hull House became a complex of buildings. An art gallery, a gymnasium, a playground—all these were added by people who believed in Jane Addams. Able volunteers came to carry on the work Jane had begun.

For Jane Addams, however, the Hull House was only a first step. As she looked around her and saw the poverty, Jane worried about the working men and women. She was especially concerned that young children were being forced to work long hours in dirty factories. Jane knew she must do even more to help. And so must others, especially the government, she thought.

Carefully she and her volunteers investigated the dreadful conditions in which the poor lived and worked and discussed how their lives could be made better. Eagerly she joined with other organizations that were trying to improve life for the poor. Even more, she began to urge government officials to pass laws that would forbid young children to hold factory jobs, would make factories safer, and would limit the working hours in a day. Inspired by Jane Addams, by her speeches and books, others, too, began to demand reforms.

Busy as she was, by 1913 Jane became involved in two other causes: women's right to vote and world peace. Even when the United States entered World War I, Jane boldly called for peace. Angrily, many people in the country spoke against her. Why didn't she support her country as it fought, they wondered.

She was hurt that so many of her supporters turned away from her. But she would not be silent. Eventually she joined with women around the world to form a women's peace organization, and she served as its leader for fourteen years. Finally, in 1931, her work for peace was recognized throughout the world—Jane Addams was awarded the Nobel Peace Prize.

Now honored and respected by millions, Jane spent the final years of her life doing what she had always done, helping others at Hull House. Busy at her tasks, she was one day suddenly taken ill. A short time later, on May 31, 1935, Jane Addams passed away.

Unwilling to do what so many single women of her day were doing—spending quiet hours at home—Jane had led a different life. She had had a dream and worked to make it a reality. Through her dedication and hard work, she had inspired and led others to voice their concerns for the poor. Children and adults, workers and presidents had come to believe in her, had come to share her vision of a better world.

From *Notable Women*, by Arlene J. Morris-Lipsman, Copyright © 1990 Scott, Foresman and Company.

FOR DISCUSSION

1. Why do you think Jane Addams did not know how to help the poor people at first?

2. Why do you suppose the neighbors did not immediately rush to Hull House when it first opened its doors?

3. Jane believed that it was the government's job to help the poor working people. Do you agree or disagree? Explain your answer.

4. Why do you think Jane continued to speak out for peace even when her supporters were turning away from her? Can you think of a time in your own life when you, too, stood up for a cause no one else believed in? How did you feel? How do you think Jane felt?

QUOTABLE QUOTES

In 1935 the Secretary of the Interior, Harold L. Ickes, said, "Jane Addams has dared to believe that the Declaration of Independence and the Constitution of the United States were written in good faith. She is the truest American that I have ever known, and there have been none braver." What do you think Mr. Ickes's words meant? In what ways did Jane show she believed in the Declaration and the Constitution?

ACTIVITIES

1. You have just read about how Jane Addams established America's first settlement house and how she helped her neighbors. Now imagine that you and a group of your friends have decided to open a settlement house today. Like Jane, you will live in a big house that stands among smaller ones in a poor, run-down neighborhood, and you will offer help to your neighbors in any way you can.

Think about the kinds of things Jane did for the people who lived near Hull House. Now within your group, think about and discuss the kinds of programs you might sponsor to better the lives of your neighbors. List your ideas on separate sheets of paper.

Now discuss specific plans for each program. What kinds of things will you do? For instance, if you have decided to organize a boys' club, will you go on field trips? Where will you go? Will you have sports teams? What sports will you play? List your detailed plans on each sheet of paper under each program title.

When you have finished planning your settlement house, collect your papers and put them together to form a book. Now share your ideas by passing your book along to the other groups in your class.

2. When Jane Addams began to demand reforms in working conditions, many criticisms were directed toward her, especially by factory owners and government officials in Chicago.

In class, count off by 2's. The number 1's will imagine they are Jane Addams. The number 2's will imagine they are factory owners.

Now, imagine that the year is 1900 and that television existed. Television then, as today, might have given the public a chance to speak out and present opinions on a subject.

Think about Jane Addams's demand for reforms and write a short commentary (speech expressing an opinion). Remember, if you are a factory owner, you are against them and if you are Jane Addams, you are for them.

Now, when you have finished your commentaries, present them to your "television audience" (your classmates).

Two speakers at a time (one factory worker, the other Jane Addams) should sit at the front of the room. The factory owner will present his commentary first. Jane Addams will follow with an opposing point of view.

Think about each commentary as it is delivered. Which point of view makes the most sense?

FOR FURTHER RESEARCH

1. Find out more about some of Jane Addams's able group of volunteers—Florence Kelley, for example. How did Jane inspire Florence? What did Florence do both with Jane and on her own to better conditions for the working poor?

2. Find out if settlement houses ever existed in your area. What services did they offer the community? How were they similar to Hull House? Do settlement houses still exist today? Is there a need for them today? What other community institutions are there today that are similar to the settlement house?

REFORMS ARE NECESSARY.

3. During Jane Addams's time, children were forced to work long hard hours in factories. Find out more about the child labor laws that protect the rights of children today. When were these laws passed? Did Jane Addams influence the passage of any of these laws? What kinds of work are children not permitted to do?

FOR FURTHER READING

Brin, Ruth. *Contributions of Women: Social Reform.* Minneapolis, Minn., Dillon Press, 1977, pp. 55-75.

Gilbert, Miriam. *Jane Addams: World Neighbor.* New York: Abingdon Press, 1960.

Mooney, Elizabeth Comstock. *Jane Addams.* Chicago: Follett, 1968.

Mary McLeod Bethune

Educator
1875–1955

MARY MCLEOD BETHUNE BEGAN HER LIFE as a cotton picker. By the time she died, she had talked with presidents and was famous throughout the United States. How did she become such an important national figure?

Nine-year-old Mary Jane McLeod gazed around the crowded playroom. Spying a book, she picked it up and began to look through the pages. Her white playmate snatched the book from her and rudely told Mary that books were only for people who could read. Unable to hold back her tears, Mary, who spent the days working in her father's cotton field, promised herself that one day she would learn to read.

In the 1880s, young Mary finally had her chance to see her dream come true. A school for black children, the first one ever in her neighborhood, had finally opened near her home in Mayesville, South Carolina. Mary's parents agreed that she could attend.

Not only did Mary graduate from that small, neighborhood school, she won a scholarship to continue her education, first at Scotia Seminary in North Carolina and later at the Moody Bible College in Chicago.

Concerned about her future, Mary eventually accepted a teaching position in Georgia. Much to her surprise, she discovered she loved teaching. Even after she had married Albertus Bethune and had had a child, Mary was not content to stay at home and be a wife and mother. She wanted to help black people by teaching them. Even more, she dreamed of starting a school of her own.

Moving now to Florida, Mrs. Bethune (only her close friends were permitted to call her Mary) began to make her dream come true. Soon she had found the perfect spot to open her school—Daytona.

She had only $1.50 in her purse. But by asking friends, neighbors, even strangers for contributions, Mrs. Bethune raised enough money to rent an old run-down house to use as her school building.

On October 3, 1904 Mrs. Bethune was warmly welcoming her first five young students to the Daytona Educational and Industrial School for Negro Girls. Within two years, two hundred and fifty black girls were attending classes. And in 1907 Mrs. Bethune raised money to buy land and built an even bigger building for her school.

The school grew, and eventually Mrs. Bethune joined it with the all-male Cookman Institute. In 1925 she became president of this newly created Bethune-Cookman College.

By now, Mrs. Bethune was becoming recognized as a leader among black people. Active in several black organizations, she spoke out on behalf of her people, calling for racial equality and better opportunities for blacks. Although she herself often faced prejudice, she was becoming a symbol of what a black person could achieve.

As time passed, Mrs. Bethune looked for even more ways to help her people, as black Americans were suffering worse hardships than ever before. The Great Depression had hit America hard, leaving people hungry, homeless, and jobless.

During these desperate times, however, one black leader stood out among her people offering hope for the future: Mary McLeod Bethune. She was first appointed by President Franklin Roosevelt to the advisory committee of the National Youth Administration. Later she was put in charge of the Office of Minority Affairs. In this new role, Mrs. Bethune helped create and find jobs for both students and unemployed young people.

As an important black leader, Mrs. Bethune eventually accepted another government assignment. In 1945, when the United Nations was being created, she was selected to attend a conference of men and women who would be organizing the new world body. As a consultant and adviser, Mrs. Bethune was concerned that people throughout the world, especially minority peoples, would be well treated.

Even after her United Nations assignment was completed, Mrs. Bethune kept busy. She was older now and more often sickly and tired. Still, she continued to speak out and fight for her people. The day came, however, when she could no longer fight. She died on May 19, 1955.

Because Mary McLeod Bethune had cared enough, young black people, now grown, were making their own way in the world. She had started her life only wanting to read. She had ended that life serving mankind and bettering the lives of all those around her.

FOR DISCUSSION

1. Why did you think Mary was unable to read even though she was nine years old?

2. Mrs. Bethune could have helped her people simply by being a teacher. Why do you think she wanted to establish a school of her own?

3. Why do you think so many people—blacks and whites—contributed money to Mrs. Bethune's school?

4. Although Mrs. Bethune was famous, she still faced prejudice. Why do you think this was so?

5. Mrs. Bethune was quite busy running her school. Why do you think, then, that she accepted government assignments?

QUOTABLE QUOTES

In her will, Mrs. Bethune wrote about what she was leaving her countrymen."I leave you love; I leave you hope; I leave you a thirst for education; I leave you faith; I leave you racial dignity; I leave you a desire to live harmoniously with your fellow men; I leave you, finally, a responsibility to our young people." Why do you think Mrs. Bethune gave these gifts to her fellow Americans? In what ways did she give these same gifts even when she was living?

ACTIVITIES

1. Mary McLeod Bethune spent the early days of her career teaching. Not only did she love her work, she was also bettering the lives of black people.

Imagine now that you are Mrs. Bethune and that you are beginning your teaching career. As a teacher, you must prepare a lesson to teach to your students. Develop a short lesson (about ten minutes long), on whatever subject you wish, to present to your classmates. You may use textbooks, newspapers, or magazines to help you select a lesson. You may also make up your own lesson based on your own knowledge.

Think about the information you will present. How will you explain it? Will you need a chalkboard or other aids to help your students understand the lesson?

When you have finished teaching your lesson, be sure to ask your classmates if they have any questions.

2. Imagine that you have just written a book about the life of Mary McLeod Bethune. To complete your book, you must design a book jacket for it.

First paste two pieces of construction paper together so that they make one large sheet of paper. Next, fold over each end of the paper to make a wide flap. Now fold the paper down the middle. Finally, take two sheets of lined paper and cut them so that they will fit on the flaps. Paste the sheets of paper onto the flaps.

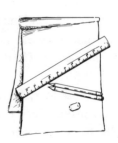

On the lined sheets of paper, write two or three paragraphs (in your own words) summing up the life of Mrs. Bethune. Include only the major details of her life. (Your job is to get your readers interested enough so that they will want to read the entire book.) Be sure to include a few sentences that will explain why Mrs. Bethune was such a notable woman.

When you have finished, paste another sheet of lined paper on the back cover of your book jacket. Write a paragraph or two about yourself, and title it "About the Author."

To complete your book jacket, draw a picture on the front cover that tells something about Mrs. Bethune's life. Also include a title for your book.

When everyone has finished his or her book jackets, display them around the room.

FOR FURTHER RESEARCH

1. Find out more about the Bethune-Cookman College that Mrs. Bethune established. What kind of college is it? What kinds of courses are offered?

2. Find out more about Mrs. Bethune's United Nations assignment. What programs did she suggest? How did she help put her suggestions into practice?

3. Find out more about the two Depression era programs for which Mrs. Bethune worked—the National Youth Administration and the Office of Minority Affairs. How did these two programs work? How did they help young people?

FOR FURTHER READING

Carruth, Ella Kaiser. *The Story of Mary McLeod Bethune: She Wanted to Read*. New York: Abingdon Press, 1966.

Fleming, Alice. *Great Women Teachers*. Philadelphia: J. B. Lippincott Company, 1965, pp. 71–85.

McKissack, Patricia. *Mary McLeod Bethune: A Great American Educator*. Chicago: Childrens Press, 1985.

Eleanor Roosevelt

Humanitarian
1884–1962

ELEANOR ROOSEVELT WAS ONE OF AMERICA'S FIRST LADIES, but as she neared the end of her life, she became known as "First Lady of the World." What did Eleanor do to earn this title?

For the first time in years, Eleanor Roosevelt was happy. Here at school in England, painful thoughts of her father and mother, dead by the time she was ten, were pushed to the back of her mind. Slowly she began to forget the sad, lonely life she had led at her grandmother's house.

When she returned to New York in 1902, it was to a new start in life. Eighteen-year-old Eleanor Roosevelt had fallen in love—with her distant cousin Franklin Roosevelt. Three years later, she and Franklin were married.

Eleanor spent the next fifteen years trying to be a good wife and mother. When the United States entered World War I, however, she wanted to help her country. Eagerly she jumped into volunteer work. She even helped to organize a Navy Red Cross. As she busied herself with her duties, Eleanor began to feel a need to help suffering people. Even more, she was slowly becoming an independent woman.

With the end of the war, Eleanor Roosevelt became actively involved in community affairs. She was now especially interested in women's concerns. Joining the League of

Women Voters, she spent much of her time attending meetings, writing reports, and talking about the problems women faced.

Eleanor was also becoming involved in politics. By 1928 she had become a well-respected leader in the Women's Division of the New York State Democratic Committee. Traveling throughout New York, she spoke at women's gatherings and raised money for the Democratic party.

When her husband became governor of New York in 1928, Eleanor was even busier. Now she toured prisons and hospitals, inspecting conditions and reporting her findings to her husband.

At last she was doing something to help people. Was it enough, though, she wondered. For by now the country was in the midst of the Great Depression. Millions of Americans had already lost their jobs. Just as many were either hungry or homeless. But, she asked herself, what could one woman do?

In 1932 Eleanor had the opportunity to answer this question. Franklin had just been elected president of the United States. Other First Ladies, Eleanor knew, had been nothing more than hostesses, entertaining luncheon and dinner guests. She would not be that kind of First Lady, she decided. She would instead be herself.

To Eleanor that meant helping people. Traveling throughout the country, she visited slums and hospitals, industrial plants and coal mines. Everywhere she went, she talked to people—everyday, ordinary people. Returning to Washington, D.C., she told Franklin about the suffering she had seen. She urged him to help these desperate people.

Eleanor also answered thousands of the letters she received, letters from people begging for help. She spoke to the crowds, talking about the needs of the poor, the needs of women. In a time when too few cared, Eleanor even spoke out for the rights of blacks.

She was admired by millions, but she was also criticized. Eleanor, some said, had no business concerning herself with the country's problems.

These words hurt her, but Eleanor just couldn't stop helping people. When the United States entered World War II in 1941, she added another job to her list of duties—visiting soldiers in Europe and the Pacific Islands.

In 1945, however, Eleanor's work suddenly came to a crashing halt. President Franklin Roosevelt died. Leaving Washington, Eleanor believed her work was over.

The new president, Harry Truman, had other ideas, though. In 1945 he asked Eleanor to represent the United States at the first meeting of the newly formed United Nations. Believing deeply in world peace and cooperation, Eleanor served with the United Nations for seven years. During that time, she led a committee that wrote the United Nations Declaration of Human Rights.

Although she was now getting on in years, she kept busy traveling and talking to world leaders and everyday people. By 1962, however, she had become quite ill. On November 7, 1962, Eleanor Roosevelt passed away.

She had spent over forty-five years helping her fellow Americans, and then she had spent the final years of her life dedicated to world peace. She had given of herself to others because she had believed in humankind, believed in the dignity of the human being.

FOR DISCUSSION

1. Why do you think Eleanor spent the first fifteen years of her married life simply trying to be a good wife and mother instead of trying to be an independent woman?

2. Why do you think Eleanor became concerned about women's problems and issues?

3. Although Eleanor was involved in politics, she never ran for office. Why do you think this was so?

4. Why do you think Eleanor was not content to be the hostess of the White House? What conditions in this country and in the world made it possible for her to be a more active First Lady? By the 1930s and 1940s how had women's roles changed?

5. Why do you think President Truman selected Eleanor as a representative to the United Nations? What kind of qualities do you think she had in order to be able to do her job so well?

QUOTABLE QUOTES

Adlai Stevenson once said about Eleanor Roosevelt, "She would rather light a candle than curse the darkness. And her glow has warmed the world." What do you think these words mean? Give examples of things Mrs. Roosevelt did which illustrate this quote.

ACTIVITIES

1. One of Eleanor Roosevelt's greatest achievements was chairing the United Nations committee that eventually wrote the Declaration of Human Rights.

As a class, suggest some ideas on what the term "Declaration of Human Rights" might mean. List your ideas on the chalkboard.

Now divide into small groups. Imagine that the year is 1946 and that you are a delegate to the United Nations. (You may represent any country you wish.) You and the other members of your group have just been selected by United Nations officials to write a Declaration of Human Rights.

First choose one person to act as chairperson of your committee. This person will represent Eleanor Roosevelt. The chairperson will open and close the meeting, explain its purpose, and call on members to speak.

Before you begin, review in your mind what the words "Declaration of Human Rights" mean. Then, within your group, discuss what rights you think all human beings are entitled to, no matter where they live. After you have presented all your ideas, choose the five rights you think are the most important. Print these five human rights on a large sheet of paper. Head your paper with the title "Declaration of Human Rights."

When all the groups have finished their lists, share them by displaying them around the room.

2. During the time Eleanor Roosevelt was First Lady, she had both admirers and critics. Think about why people might have admired Eleanor and why they might have criticized her.

From *Notable Women*, by Arlene J. Morris-Lipsman, Copyright © 1990 Scott, Foresman and Company.

Within your classroom divide into groups of six. In your group, choose one team of three people (Team A) who will represent Eleanor's admirers and one team of three people (Team B) who will represent her critics. Within your team discuss your reasons for either admiring Eleanor (Team A) or criticizing her (Team B) and list the reasons on a sheet of paper. Next, as a team, present your reasons for admiring or criticizing Eleanor in a written paragraph. Be sure to begin your paragraph with a topic sentence.

Now choose one person from each team to read the paragraphs aloud to each other. Team A will go first. After the paragraphs have been read, think about what your opposing team has said. Do you disagree with its presentation? Do you have any questions you'd like to ask the other team? All three members of your team will now have the opportunity to comment or to question your opponents. Team A will again go first.

FOR FURTHER RESEARCH

1. Find out more about one other important First Lady, Abigail Adams. In what ways was she like Eleanor Roosevelt? In what ways was she different?

2. Find out more about Eleanor Roosevelt's work with the United Nations. What were some of her important accomplishments?

3. Find out more about Eleanor's travels throughout the world during the 1950s. With which important world leaders did she speak?

FOR FURTHER READING

Faber, Dorie. *Eleanor Roosevelt: First Lady of the World.* New York: Viking Kestrel, 1986.

Jacobs, William Jay. *Eleanor Roosevelt: A Life of Happiness and Tears.* New York: Coward-McCann, 1983.

Whitney, Sharon. *Eleanor Roosevelt.* New York: Franklin Watts, 1982.

Mother Teresa

Humanitarian
1910–

MOTHER TERESA BECAME A SYMBOL TO NEEDY PEOPLE throughout the world. What did Mother Teresa symbolize?

As a child, Agnes Gonxha Bojaxhiu was worried. No one cared about the poor, sick, and homeless people of India. One day, the young Yugoslavian child told herself, she would help them.

When Agnes was eighteen, she made up her mind. She would join the Sisters of Loreto and become a nun. Like the other Sisters, she would go to India as a missionary. There she would serve God by doing good deeds and by spreading His love among the people.

Agnes tearfully said goodbye to her family and friends in Skope, Yugoslavia. Then she boarded the train that would take her far away from her home. After a short stay in Ireland, Agnes began her journey to India.

For two years she lived in the city of Darjeeling, learning the life of a nun. At this time, Agnes also chose a new name for herself. She would be called Teresa in honor of a Catholic saint.

Sister Teresa was sent to Calcutta to teach in a Catholic school, St. Mary's. For many years she taught geography and history to young girls. Then she became principal of the school. For a long time she loved her work and was happy.

During all this time, however, Sister Teresa never forgot her dream of working with the poor. Just outside the school was one of Calcutta's worst slums. No one else seemed to care about the people who lived there. But Sister Teresa did.

One day when Sister Teresa was worrying about the poor, she suddenly knew what she had to do. She must leave St. Mary's and go live among the poor. She would live simply, as they did, and help them.

And so, in 1948 Sister Teresa left St. Mary's. She went first to a hospital in Patna so she could learn how to care for the sick. Then she returned to Calcutta, where she went directly to the slums. She gathered a few children together. Then she began to teach them. She used the dirt as her chalkboard.

Sister Teresa also helped the sick people. She gave them medicine and nursed them. Soon many people in India learned about Sister Teresa's work. Some of the students from St. Mary's came to help her. People began to send her food and supplies for the needy.

Sister Teresa's group of women came to be known as the Missionaries of Charity, and she herself was now being called Mother Teresa.

Mother Teresa was very busy, but she believed she must do even more for the people. All around her she saw poor, dying people. No one wanted to take them in, not even the hospitals. Mother Teresa decided to open a special home just to take care of the dying.

Mother Teresa also worried about the poor, abandoned children. Soon she had opened another home, this one for children. She loved these children and took care of them. She even helped many of them find homes with loving families.

Her work was not finished, though. Now Mother Teresa wanted to help people who were suffering from a disease called leprosy. Everyone feared and avoided these people. In time, Mother Teresa opened a home for lepers. She and the other nuns cared for them when no one else would.

Now people from all over the world were hearing about Mother Teresa's work. They sent supplies and money to help her. Mother Teresa didn't use the money for herself. She used it to help her people.

More women, and men too, were joining her. People everywhere asked Mother Teresa to start a Missionaries of Charity in their country. She agreed, and today her missionaries are found on five continents throughout the world.

In 1979 Mother Teresa received a great honor. She was awarded the Nobel Peace Prize because of her work with the needy.

Mother Teresa had fulfilled her childhood dream. She had offered love and caring to people who needed it most. This woman who only wanted to help others became a symbol of hope to people everywhere throughout the world.

FOR DISCUSSION

1. What qualities do you think it was necessary for Agnes to have in order to be a good missionary?

2. After she had left St. Mary's and had studied in Patna, Sister Teresa returned to Calcutta. She went directly to the slums. What is a slum? How can slums exist even in cities and countries in which there is great wealth and advanced technology?

3. Mother Teresa helped the sick, the dying, the homeless, the children, and the lepers. Why do you think she helped so many different groups of people instead of focusing on just one group?

4. Why do you think people from all over the world sent money and supplies to Mother Teresa?

5. Mother Teresa does not wear fancy clothes, nor does she eat big, filling meals. Instead she lives simply, like the people she helps. Why do you think Mother Teresa has chosen to live like this? How has her decision to live like the poor affected her work?

QUOTABLE QUOTES

Mother Teresa once said, "We ourselves feel that what we are doing is just a drop in the ocean. But if that drop was not in the ocean I think that the ocean will be less because of that missing drop." What do these words mean to you? How has Mother Teresa demonstrated her feelings through her work?

ACTIVITIES

1. Wearing her thin cotton dress (sari), Mother Teresa accepted the Nobel Peace Prize. As she spoke to the audience, her words reflected her strong beliefs and feelings about "her people."

Imagine that you are Mother Teresa and you have just been called upon to deliver a speech for receiving the Nobel Peace Prize. What would you say?

Prepare a speech that Mother Teresa might have presented to the audience. Think about the beliefs that were important to her. Think about what the prize would mean to a woman like Mother Teresa. Think about why the money she received would be important to her. Be sure to include these ideas in your speech.

When you have finished writing your speech, present it to your classmates. As you speak, imagine how Mother Teresa would have spoken. Would she have read her words in a loud, clear voice or in a soft one? Would she have smiled at her audience or would her face have been serious? How would she have stood? Deliver your speech as you think Mother Teresa would have.

2. Think about the following events that occurred in Mother Teresa's life:

- She left her family and friends in Skope, Yugoslavia forever.
- She took her final vows to become a nun.
- She asked the head of her church for permission to leave St. Mary's to work with the needy.
- She spoke with the other young women who wanted to join her in her work.
- She gathered the children of the slums together in order to teach them.
- She found a woman lying on the street dying.
- She talked to the lepers everyone feared and avoided.

Divide the class into groups. Within your group choose one of the above situations. Prepare a short skit to act out this event. As you write your script, think about what the characters, especially Mother Teresa, might have actually said and how they would have felt.

When you have finished your script, present your skit to your classmates. As you act out your parts, remember to think, feel, and speak as the characters you are portraying would have.

FOR FURTHER RESEARCH

1. Mother Teresa works in India. Locate India on your world map or globe. On what continent is India? Now find out more about India. What people live there? What are living conditions like for many of these people? Why are so many people forced to live in poverty? Why is there a need for the kind of work Mother Teresa does? What else did you learn about India?

2. In what other countries can Missionaries of Charity be found? Find out more about these countries. What conditions exist in these countries that qualify them for Mother Teresa's work?

3. Find out more about other Nobel Peace Prize winners. Were any of them women? For what kind of work did they receive the prize? Compare their work to Mother Teresa's. How is it similar? How is it different?

FOR FURTHER READING

Green, Carol. *Mother Teresa: Friend of the Friendless.* Chicago: Childrens Press, 1983.

Lee, Betsy. *Mother Teresa: Caring for All God's Children.* Minneapolis, Minn.: Dillon Press, 1981.

Leigh, Vanora. *Mother Teresa.* New York: Bookwright Press, 1986.

From *Notable Women,* by Arlene J. Morris-Lipsman, Copyright © 1990 Scott, Foresman and Company.

Betty Friedan

Feminist
1921–

I N THE MINDS OF MANY, BETTY FRIEDAN, a suburban housewife and mother, was responsible for starting a revolution. What was this revolution about? How did it begin?

The teenaged Betty Goldstein sighed. How she longed to join the sorority (a private girls' club). How she wished she were asked out on dates. But she was not. She knew why, of course. She was Jewish—an outsider as far as her high school classmates were concerned. Prejudice against minorities, unfair treatment—yes, thought Betty, she understood it well. She would understand it for the rest of her life.

By the time she entered Smith College, however, Betty Goldstein was no longer pitying herself. Instead, she was busy writing for the school paper and eagerly sharing in discussions with her teachers and friends about world affairs.

After earning an advanced degree in psychology, Betty Goldstein moved to New York, where she eventually met Carl Friedan. And when in 1947 they were married and Betty was expecting her first child, her life became complete—or at least that's what she thought.

Marriage and children—that was what every woman was taught to want. Women's magazines and psychologists agreed. A woman could only be happy if she were married and stayed at home to raise her children. As she read and listened to the experts, Betty nodded her head. Yes, it made sense.

Betty began to live the kind of life women were supposed to live, ordinary days filled with household chores and caring for her children. When did the dissatisfaction begin? Betty hardly knew. She only knew that she was restless, terribly restless, and she wanted to do more. What was wrong with her, Betty wondered. Why was she so unhappy?

In just a short while, in 1956, Betty would learn that other women shared her dissatisfaction. Invited by Smith College to do a survey of her former classmates, Betty Friedan asked questions. How were other women adjusting to their lives as wives and mothers? The answers she received shocked her. Like Betty, these other women longed to do something more with their lives.

Now Betty really began to investigate women's lives. She interviewed them and she talked to psychologists and guidance counselors, too. She wrote about her findings in a book, *The Feminine Mystique*, which was published in 1963.

As Betty explained it to her readers, the feminine mystique was the belief that women should not want either an education or a career. They should only want to be housewives and mothers. Disagreeing, Betty advised women that they should want more. They should have more.

As *The Feminine Mystique* became a bestseller, women throughout the United States talked about Betty's book. As for Betty Friedan, now divorced from her husband, she had only just begun to speak out for women. Women must be able to pursue worthwhile careers, she told all who would listen. Even more, these working women must have the same advantages as men—equal pay, equal opportunities to be hired, equal chance for promotion.

But how could women make this happen, Betty wondered. Perhaps a national women's organization might help. And so, in 1966, Betty Friedan and several other feminist leaders formed the National Organization for Women (NOW).

As president of NOW, Betty began to push for laws that would make women equal to men. She demanded that women be included in government, in businesses, even in history books.

As NOW grew, so did Betty's plans for action. In 1970 she headed a Women's Strike for Equality, and on August 26 thousands of eager women marched through city streets in a demonstration of unity and a call for equality.

Even after Betty resigned as president of NOW (in 1970), she continued to speak out for women. She wrote books and magazine articles and gave lectures to people all over the world. Always, Betty Friedan's message remained clear and unchanged. Women were people, too—people who deserved the chance to be someone.

By the mid-1980s, Betty Friedan, the "mother of the women's movement," could look back through the years and smile a bit in satisfaction. Women were taking their places in government, universities, and businesses.

It had been a long and difficult struggle, this fight for equal rights. Still, thought Betty, so much remained to be done. She at last understood. The revolution had only just begun.

FOR DISCUSSION

1. Why do you think Betty felt that something was wrong with her when she began to want more out of life?

2. Why do you think women living in the 1950s were taught to believe that they could only find happiness by caring for their husbands and children?

3. Why do you think Betty decided to share her feelings with other women in *The Feminine Mystique*?

4. While many women agreed with *The Feminine Mystique*, just as many did not. Why do you think this was so? Do you agree with the ideas Betty Friedan presented in *The Feminine Mystique*? Explain your answer.

5. Betty Friedan was a woman who dared to speak out about women's lives even when no one else would. Why do you suppose so few other women talked about women's problems?

6. Writing *The Feminine Mystique* was not enough for Betty Friedan. She also began to push for better laws for women. What laws for women do you think are necessary and should be passed?

QUOTABLE QUOTES

Betty Friedan wrote of her decision to start the National Organization for Women, "Yes, we knew what we were doing. We couldn't possibly know where it would lead, but we knew what had to be done. But why me, why us? Who wants to take the responsibility, to commit oneself to carry it through, and risk being laughed at, getting people mad at you, maybe getting fired?" Why do you think Betty Friedan was willing to take these risks despite the consequences? In your own experiences, when have you been willing to take a risk, to stand up for what you believe in, despite the consequences? How did you feel in the situation? How do you think Betty felt? Why is it important to stand up for your beliefs?

ACTIVITIES

1. When Betty Friedan first organized the National Organization for Women, she had to make sure that women throughout the United States would be aware of what she was doing. How do you think she was able to make women aware of her plan?

Imagine that you have been asked to organize a NOW chapter in your school. You would like to invite as many students as possible to attend your first meeting. How will you do this?

Within your class divide into small groups. In your group discuss some ways you can publicize or make your meeting known. Will you make posters? Will you write an article for your school newspaper about the meeting? What else can you do?

After you have discussed your plan of action, prepare an actual publicity campaign—a series of advertisement buttons and bumper stickers that will let

From *Notable Women*, by Arlene J. Morris-Lipsman, Copyright © 1990 Scott, Foresman and Company.

the students know about your planned meeting and draw interest to NOW. Decide what each person in the group will do to advertise the meeting. Then create the actual materials you will use to publicize your meeting.

When you have finished preparing your materials, share them with your classmates by presenting them in a brief oral report. Be prepared to explain what you have done to advertise the meeting.

2. With the start of the women's movement, job opportunities in all fields became more available to women. Think about the kinds of work women were now able to do. Within your class, talk about some of these newly opened career choices, and list them on the chalkboard.

Now imagine that you are writing a book for young girls about career opportunities for women. Think about what careers you would like to include.

Using separate sheets of paper, draw pictures that will represent each career. To do this, you may want to include some of the equipment used in each job. You might want to use a number of different materials (cloth, paste sticks, aluminum foil, etc.) to make your pictures seem more realistic. When you have completed each picture, title it and then write a few sentences explaining the career.

When you have finished your pictures, put them together to make a book. Remember to include a front cover that lists the title of your book.

Now share your books with classmates by displaying them around the room.

FOR FURTHER RESEARCH

1. Find out more about the National Organization for Women. What are some of its current issues? Who are some of its leaders? You may want to find out if there is a NOW chapter in your city. What kinds of activities has it participated in?

2. Find out more about ERA, the Equal Rights Amendment. If it is passed, what rights will it guarantee? Why have some women supported the ERA and others not? Why has the ERA had so much difficulty in getting passed?

3. Find out more about another woman involved in the fight for equal rights: Gloria Steinem. In what ways was her work similar to Betty Friedan's? In what ways was it different?

FOR FURTHER READING

Melzer, Milton. *Betty Friedan: A Voice for Women's Rights.* New York: Viking Kestrel, 1987.

THINKING IT OVER

1. Jane Addams believed that the government must help the poor working people, and she urged it to make needed reforms. In what ways does today's United States government help the underprivileged?

2. Jane Addams believed in peace no matter what the cost. In what ways are today's world powers trying to ensure world peace?

3. Why is it important that black Americans serve in government positions? Can you name any other black Americans who have served in the United States government?

4. What does the United Nations stand for? Do you think the world needs an organization like the United Nations? Explain your answer.

5. Think about people in your community who help the poor, sick, and homeless. Identify some of these groups of people. How do they help the needy? How is their work like Mother Teresa's? How is it different?

6. Susan B. Anthony and Betty Friedan both fought for a similar cause. Compare their experiences as they sought to make their dreams come true. How were they alike? Which woman do you think made more of an impact on the lives of other women? Why do you think this was so?

8. Like Harriet Tubman, Mary McLeod Bethune wanted to help her people. In what ways was Mrs. Bethune's experiences different from Harriet Tubman's? What advantages did Mrs. Bethune have that Harriet Tubman didn't have?

9. Jane Addams, Eleanor Roosevelt, and Mother Teresa all dedicated their lives to helping poor people. Which woman do you think was more readily accepted by her society? Why do you think this was so? Which woman do you think faced the most obstacles as she attempted to help the underprivileged? Explain your answer.

MEDICINE

Elizabeth Blackwell

Physician
1821–1910

ELIZABETH BLACKWELL STARTLED HER FAMILY AND FRIENDS when she announced her choice of a career. What had Elizabeth decided to become? Why were people so stunned by her decision?

Even when she was a young girl, Elizabeth Blackwell was different from her friends. Unlike them, she was busily studying math, history, Greek, and Latin. In the 1820s, this was unheard of. Most people thought that girls should not be educated. Elizabeth, however, loved learning. The more she learned, the more she wanted to know.

She continued her studies even after her family moved from England to America. By the time she was fourteen, Elizabeth was already thinking about her future. She would do something with her life, she decided, something no other woman had done.

When she was eighteen, Elizabeth and her sisters opened a school for girls. Teaching was one of the few acceptable ways for a woman to earn a living in those days. However, Elizabeth soon discovered that she disliked teaching. When the sisters finally closed the school, Elizabeth breathed a sigh of relief.

One hot summer afternoon, twenty-four-year-old Elizabeth Blackwell went to visit a sick friend. The friend wondered aloud why women shouldn't be doctors. She believed that a woman like Elizabeth, for example, would make an excellent doctor.

From *Notable Women*, by Arlene J. Morris-Lipsman, Copyright © 1990 Scott, Foresman and Company.

Elizabeth thought hard about that conversation. Suddenly, she knew what she would do. She would become America's first woman doctor.

Once Elizabeth made up her mind, no one could change it. But Elizabeth realized she had to face a big problem. Would any medical school admit a woman, she wondered?

Elizabeth developed a plan. First she would study privately with doctors who were already established. Then, when she had learned enough, she would apply to medical school.

At first she could not find a doctor who was willing to train her. Women could not be doctors, they told her. Finally, Elizabeth found some doctors who agreed to help her.

Getting into medical school was a lot more difficult. She applied to many and was turned down by all of them. At last, in 1847, Geneva Medical College in New York agreed to accept Elizabeth Blackwell as a student. She looked forward to starting her studies.

In the beginning, it was hard for Elizabeth. The townspeople criticized her or ignored her. Who was this woman who dared to be different, they wondered?

Even her teachers and fellow students didn't know what to make of Elizabeth. But because she was a good student, they soon accepted her. Two years later, in 1849, a proud Elizabeth received her medical diploma.

Elizabeth decided to continue her studies in Europe. At last, in 1851, she returned to New York. She was ready to practice medicine.

At first she had no patients. People just wouldn't trust a woman doctor. Finally, a few patients began to trickle in. Word spread that Elizabeth Blackwell was indeed a good doctor. Her practice grew.

Soon Elizabeth grew restless. She needed to do more. She wanted to open a hospital for poor women and children. She was able to raise the money she needed, and on May 1, 1857 the hospital opened its doors.

Elizabeth's fame was spreading rapidly. She was now accepted as a doctor, but she wanted to help other women who dreamed of entering the field of medicine. She decided to start a medical school for women. They would be taught and trained at her own hospital. In 1866 she opened her school. Soon women doctors were becoming accepted throughout the country. Elizabeth Blackwell had paved the way for them.

Things were running smoothly, but Elizabeth was soon restless again. She needed more challenges. She decided to go to England where, years ago, she had been recognized as the first woman doctor in that country. She would help other English women become accepted as doctors.

For a while, that's what Elizabeth did. She was getting older, though, and she was feeling tired. She decided to retire and spend her time writing books on medicine.

Elizabeth lived quietly in retirement until May 31, 1910, when she died peacefully.

In her lifetime, Elizabeth Blackwell had become an inspiration for women throughout the world, opening many previously locked doors. She had taught them that women could indeed be more if they really tried.

FOR DISCUSSION

1. Elizabeth Blackwell was taught that an education was important. However, in the 1820s, most people felt that girls should not be educated. Why do you think they believed this?

2. All her life, Elizabeth was different from other women. Given what you know about Elizabeth, do you think being different bothered Elizabeth? Why?

3. When Elizabeth was a teenager and young adult, she knew she wanted to do something with her life, but she didn't really know exactly what. Why do you think she was so undecided? What opportunities were open to women at that time?

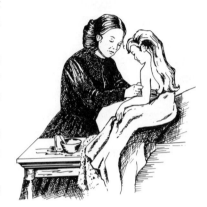

4. How did the townspeople treat Elizabeth once they knew she was going to medical school? How would you characterize these people? If you were to meet them, what would you say to them?

5. Elizabeth was never content to rest on her achievements. She always felt the need to do more. What do you think might have motivated Elizabeth's desire to achieve as much as she could?

QUOTABLE QUOTES

Twenty years after she had graduated from college, Elizabeth Blackwell remarked, "It is not easy to be a pioneer—but oh, it is fascinating! I would not trade one moment, even the worst moment, for all the riches in the world." What are some of the problems and rewards that "pioneers" such as Elizabeth Blackwell face? Why is the word "pioneer" used to describe such people?

In addition to a person's own comments, you will often read in books and magazines comments (quotes) made *about* a famous person. If you were to write a biography about Elizabeth Blackwell, you might end your book by offering your own comments about Elizabeth. Write a quote—a sentence or two—summarizing Elizabeth Blackwell's life.

ACTIVITIES

1. Elizabeth Blackwell wrote to many medical schools applying for admission. These letters probably included not only her qualifications for admission but also reasons why she should be admitted. Although her applications were often turned down, she was finally accepted into school in part because of her qualifications.

Imagine you are Elizabeth Blackwell. Write a letter of application that you would send to medical schools. Discuss your background and why you are qualified to be accepted as a student. Also explain why you should be admitted, even though the school has never before accepted a woman student. Make your letter as convincing as possible. Remember that Elizabeth was not the usual candidate that medical schools considered.

When the class has finished their letters, divide into small groups. Each group will represent a medical school board of admissions.

Now choose students to act as Elizabeth Blackwell. These students will pass their letters to each school board. Based on the letter, each committee must decide whether it will admit Elizabeth as a student. Each committee should discuss its decision with Elizabeth, explaining why they decided as they did.

2. In 1857 Elizabeth Blackwell opened her hospital for women and children. However, much planning and problem solving were involved before the hospital became a reality.

One of the most serious problems for Elizabeth was raising the money to buy a building and equip it, for she did not have money of her own.

Imagine now that the year is 1857 and that you and your classmates have decided to open a hospital just as Elizabeth did. Like her, you have little money. Within your classroom, discuss ways that you can raise money to make your dream come true. List all your ideas on the chalkboard. When you have completed your list, discuss each idea. How well do you think each will succeed in bringing the money you need?

3. Imagine now that you have at last bought a building for your hospital. Make up a "blueprint" for your hospital. On a sheet of paper, draw a framework (an outline) of the building you will be using. Now, divide that framework into the number of rooms you will need, and label how each room will be used. Think about the furniture and equipment you will use. Where will you place them? Include them in your blueprint, too.

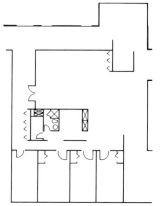

When you have finished your blueprints, share them by displaying them around the room.

FOR FURTHER RESEARCH

1. Find out about other women who have worked in the medical field. You might want to read about Elizabeth Garrott Anderson and Mary Putnam Jacobi, who were also pioneers in medicine. Think about the contributions these other women made to medicine. How did Elizabeth Blackwell pave the way for them?

2. Elizabeth Blackwell received her medical diploma after two years of studying. Today, a person who wants to become a doctor must study for more than two years. Find out more about what it takes to become a doctor today. For how long must a doctor attend school? What are some subjects today's doctors study? Do you think Elizabeth Blackwell also studied these subjects? Why?

3. Find out more about the hospitals in your area. Are any of these hospitals just for women or children? If so, find out what special types of services are provided for the patients, ones that might not be at another hospital. Why do you think some hospitals are set up to take care of women or children? Do you think Elizabeth Blackwell's ideas on caring for women and children might have influenced today's hospitals?

FOR FURTHER READING

Clapp, Patricia. *Dr. Elizabeth: The Story of the First Woman Doctor.* New York: Lothrop, Lee & Shepard, 1974.

Fox, Ruth. *Great Women of Medicine.* New York: Random House, 1964, pp. 1–47.

McFerran, Ann. *Elizabeth Blackwell: First Woman Doctor.* New York: Grosset & Dunlap, 1966.

Florence Nightingale

Nurse
1820–1910

AS A YOUNG WOMAN, Florence Nightingale dreamed of being a nurse, much to her family's dismay. By the time she died, her family would have been proud of their daughter's profession. How did Florence change the nursing profession?

Fourteen-year-old Florence Nightingale gently held the old lady's hand. Sick as she was, the woman smiled. How she appreciated Florence's visits, her tender care.

As a young woman, Florence dreamed of dedicating her life to helping poor, sick people. Perhaps she would work in a hospital as a nurse. What a useful life she would live, thought Florence.

Such an idea, however, horrified her family. In the 1840s, English hospitals were dreadful, filthy places. As for nurses, most were uneducated women who received no training in the care of the sick. No, Florence's family told her, this was no life for a wealthy, educated young woman.

The constant arguments with her family over her desire to be a nurse bothered her, but in 1851 a determined Florence made a decision. Packing her bags, she headed for Kaiserwerth, Germany to train as a nurse. By 1853 an enthusiastic Florence was working at her first job—superintendent of a private nursing home.

In 1854 Florence was searching for even greater challenges. When England declared war on Russia, Florence eagerly accepted a government assignment to lead a group of nurses who would work in the army hospital in Scutari, Turkey.

Florence was horrified at what she saw at Scutari. Row upon row of soldiers lay uncovered on the filthy floor, for there were no beds or even blankets. Medical supplies and food, too, were scarce. Worse still, the army doctors refused to accept Florence's help. She was a woman, they said—a nuisance and not wanted. Finally, however, Florence and her nurses were permitted to work.

As an administrator, she slowly made the desperately needed changes, as well as tending to the sick. She even found time to write reports to government officials describing conditions and suggesting improvements. All the while, Florence was becoming a hero—to the soldiers and to the people back home in England.

In 1856 the war was finally over, and Florence returned to England. Angry that so many soldiers had died from neglect alone, she wanted to change the entire organization of army hospitals.

When a Royal Commission was finally established to investigate and change army hospitals, Florence offered advice and suggestions. (She was not permitted to serve on the commission because she was a woman.)

Exhausted and in poor health, Florence refused to rest. There was so much more to be done—books to be written, for instance. She wrote two, one that became a guideline for building all new hospitals, and one on nursing.

Now she began to think seriously about a long-held dream of hers. Nurses received almost no respect—not from the doctors, not from the public. Florence desperately wanted to make nursing a well-respected profession.

At last, in 1860, she helped her dream come true. The Nightingale Training School officially opened its doors. Here nurses would be trained to carry out their work. Carefully, Florence chose her students. She saw to it that they followed a strict standard of behavior, and above all ensured that they received lessons in medicine.

As a result of her hard work, the school grew, and others like it were established throughout Europe and even in the United States. Nightingale nurses were everywhere, in hospitals and nursing homes, making changes in the care of the sick and earning the respect of society.

As for Florence, sick as she was and busy as she was with her school, she continued to tackle health project after project. And by now, so many people agreed: Florence Nightingale was an expert in health matters.

By 1896 Florence was too sick to even leave her bedroom. Yet she continued to work and to receive honors. In 1907 she became the first woman ever to receive England's Order of Merit.

As the days passed, Florence, blind by now, was less and less able to work. Finally, on August 13, 1910, Florence Nightingale died peacefully in her sleep.

When she was younger, nursing had been an undesirable profession, and hospitals had been places where the sick feared to go. Because of Florence Nightingale's work, hospitals were now properly tending the sick, and nurses could proudly take their place in society.

FOR DISCUSSION

1. Why do you think the army doctors considered women nurses nuisances instead of viewing them as professionals who could care for the sick and wounded?

2. By 1855 Florence had become a hero to the soldiers and to the people of England. She was one of the most admired women in English history. Why do you think this was so?

3. Despite all she had accomplished, Florence was not permitted to serve on the Royal Commission because she was a woman. Why do you think women were not permitted to work on the commission?

4. Florence chose her student nurses carefully and then insisted that they follow high standards of behavior. What qualities do you think Florence looked for in her nursing students? Of these, which three qualities do you think are most important for nurses to have? Explain.

QUOTABLE QUOTES

Novelist Elizabeth Gaskell once described Florence Nightingale: "She is so excessively soft and gentle in voice, manner, and movement that one never feels the unbendablenesss of her character when one is near her. Her powers are astonishing." What do you think Elizabeth Gaskell meant by these words? Why do you think it was necessary for Florence to be unbendable?

ACTIVITIES

1. By 1856 Florence Nightingale had become one of England's most admired women. During her two year stay at the hospital in Scutari, English people back home honored her in whatever way they could. When she announced that she was returning to England at the end of the war, even more honors were planned for her.

Imagine that the year is 1856 and that you are living in England. Like so many others, you want to honor Florence Nightingale. What would you do?

On a sheet of paper, list three ways that you could honor Florence. As you list your ideas, include an explanation of how you would put your ideas into action. Would you work independently or with a committee? Would your honor be a simple one or would it involve a good deal of preparation? Keep in mind that Florence Nightingale did not care so much for honors as she did for her patients. As you list your honors, try to include only those that you feel Florence might have accepted and enjoyed.

When the class has finished their lists, share them with one another by displaying them around the room.

From *Notable Women,* by Arlene J. Morris-Lipsman, Copyright © 1990 Scott, Foresman and Company.

2. The following words describe Florence Nightingale's character, thoughts, feelings, or actions:

daring	caring	sharing	heart	smart
part	start	brave	grave	insisted
resisted	learned	burned	tried	cried
sighed	treasures	pleasure	growing	knowing

What other words can you think of to describe Florence? Add them to the list.

Now think again about Florence Nightingale's life. Using these words or words of your own, write a two-stanza rhyming poem (four lines to a stanza) about the life of Florence Nightingale. You may choose any rhyming pattern you wish.

When everyone has finished his or her poem, share the poems with each other by reading them aloud.

FOR FURTHER RESEARCH

1. Find out more about how today's professional nurses are trained. Are they trained in hospitals or universities? You may want to interview your school nurse, the nurse who works for your family doctor, or a nurse you yourself know. You may want to look through encyclopedias or a book on nursing to find the information.

2. Florence went to Scutari to help the soldiers who were fighting in a war known as the Crimean War. There she learned about the horrors of war. Find out more about the Crimean War. Why was it fought? Who eventually won the war?

3. Find out more about today's hospitals. Your class may want to visit a hospital in your area to see how it operates. What facilities do today's hospitals provide for their patients? How have hospitals changed over the years since Florence's time?

FOR FURTHER READING

Shor, Donnali. *Why They Became Famous: Florence Nightingale.* Morristown, N.J.: Silver Burdett Company, 1986.

Turner, Dorothy. *Florence Nightingale.* New York: Bookwright Press, 1986.

Wyndham, Lee. *Florence Nightingale: Nurse to the World.* New York: World Publishing Company, 1969.

THINKING IT OVER

1. Today, is it necessary to have a medical school just for women? Why or why not? Have attitudes toward women in the medical field changed over the years? Explain your answer.

2. Elizabeth Blackwell opened the door for women in medicine. What part do women play in the medical field today? Can you give examples of women you know who are involved in the field of medicine today?

3. Today nursing is a well-respected profession. What changes have taken place in the field since the late 1800s?

4. Both Elizabeth Blackwell and Florence Nightingale were determined to make careers for themselves in the medical field. Both women faced tremendous challenges as they tried to make their dreams come true. Compare their life experiences. Which woman do you think faced more serious challenges? Why do you think this was so? In what ways were their experiences alike? In what ways did they both help change society's attitude toward women in the medical field?

ART AND LITERATURE

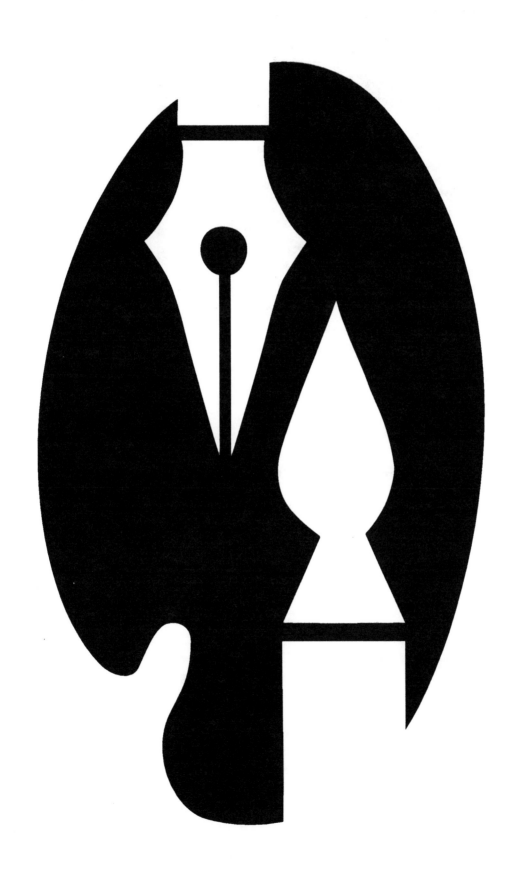

Louisa May Alcott
Author
1832–1888

FROM THE TIME SHE WAS A YOUNG GIRL, Louisa May Alcott had only one goal. With the success of her books and stories, she achieved it. What did Louisa hope to do in her lifetime?

Inside the Alcott family barn, thirteen-year-old Louisa May smiled graciously as the audience applauded the end of the play. She had been both director and star. Even more, she had written the play herself.

As she eagerly took her bows, great dreams filled Louisa's mind. One day, she thought, perhaps she would be a famous author.

Whatever the future held, Louisa was sure of one thing. She would earn enough money to support her beloved family. She, her parents, and three sisters were struggling hard just to survive. She would change that, Louisa promised herself.

When Louisa was sixteen, she opened a small school and began to teach. But busy as she was, she still found time to write. How thrilled she was when one of her stories was actually published in a magazine. And three years later, in 1855, when several of her stories were collected and published as a book, she was very proud.

At last she was an author! But Louisa was disappointed, too. She had hoped to earn enough money to support her family. Her little book just did not bring the money she longed to have.

Determined to help her family, Louisa decided to move to Boston—alone. Perhaps there she would find work suitable for a young lady.

Her neighbors were shocked by her decision. In the 1850s single young women did not leave their parents' home to look for work. Strong-willed Louisa did not care what the neighbors thought, however. In 1855 she left home and headed for Boston.

In Boston, as women did then, she taught and sewed and still she wrote. Slowly she began to sell her stories to magazines. Slowly she began to earn money.

And so the years passed. The United States had been driven into war, the great Civil War. Eagerly Louisa volunteered to help her country. She would serve as a nurse in Washington, D.C., and she would care for the sick and wounded soldiers. For several weeks, Louisa tenderly cared for her patients, until she, too, became deathly ill.

Returning to her parents' home, Louisa slowly began to recover, and soon she received news that cheered her. Letters she had written to her family about her wartime experiences were appearing in a magazine. Her "Hospital Sketches" had become so popular, in fact, that they were published in a book in 1863. And now people everywhere demanded to read more of Miss Louisa May Alcott's works.

By 1867 Louisa was already well known to magazine editors and publishers. One day, one of those publishers, Thomas Niles, asked Louisa if she would write a book for young girls. Louisa hesitated. She knew nothing about young girls, she told him. And so, for a while, Louisa forgot about Mr. Niles.

A year later, Mr. Niles repeated his request. And this time Louisa agreed.

What would she write about, she wondered? Suddenly she knew. She would write about her own family, the good times and the bad. So Louisa began to write. Quickly her pen filled the pages.

In 1868 the book, *Little Women*, was published, and Louisa instantly became famous. Young children, and adults, too, read her story. Everywhere, people loved her charming tale.

Now, at last, Louisa's childhood dreams had come true. She was a well-known author. Even more, she was finally able to support her family.

As the years passed, Louisa continued to write, story after story about young people. And she continued to delight her audiences with such books as *Little Men*, *Jo's Boys*, and *An Old-Fashioned Girl*.

Eagerly, the public now demanded her time. She answered letters, signed autographs, received visitors, and spoke at schools and colleges.

But Louisa still found time to care for her family. More and more often, though, she was tired and sick. One day in March 1888, Louisa went to visit her ailing father. On her way home, she caught a chill. Already in poor health, she fell unconscious. Two days later, on March 6, she died.

Louisa May Alcott had, for years, entertained audiences with her simple, touching tales. Over a hundred years after her death, children everywhere still eagerly pour over her words. In the hearts and minds of these young people, Louisa May Alcott has proven herself to be a gifted storyteller, a great American woman.

From *Notable Women*, by Arlene J. Morris-Lipsman, Copyright © 1990 Scott, Foresman and Company.

FOR DISCUSSION

1. Why do you think young Louisa promised herself that she would one day support her family? Considering the period of time in which she lived, why was this an unusual ambition?

2. Why do you think Louisa ignored her neighbors' opinions and moved to Boston? What difficulties and problems do you think Louisa might have faced living in Boston as a single woman?

3. During the Civil War, Louisa served her country as a nurse. Why do you think she decided to do so? Given what you know about Louisa, how do you think she felt about slavery?

4. Why do you think Louisa was asked to write a story for girls?

5. Why do you think Louisa changed her mind and decided to write this story? Why do you think her books became so popular?

QUOTABLE QUOTES

Upon her success with the sale of *Little Women*, Louisa wrote in her diary, "Paid up all the debts—every penny that money can pay—and now I feel as if I could die in peace. My dream is beginning to come true; and if my head holds out I'll do what I once hoped to do." Why do you think Louisa felt that she could die in peace because her debts were paid off? What do these words tell you about the kind of woman Louisa was?

Now imagine you are writing a book about Louisa May Alcott. How would you end your book? Write a sentence or two that would sum up her life.

ACTIVITIES

1. Although Louisa May Alcott wrote books and stories for adults, she is best remembered for her children's books. Many of these, especially *Little Women*, are based on Louisa's own experiences.

Imagine now that you are Louisa and that you have been asked to write a children's story. First, skim through the first two chapters of *Little Women* to see how Louisa told her family's story. Now think of a story you'd like to tell based on your own life. Of course, since this is fiction, you will want to change the names of your characters just as Louisa did. You may even want to change the names of places and some of the important details.

Think about an event that happened in your own life, perhaps a special adventure you shared with your family or friends. Now write a story about this event. As you tell your story, you may want to include conversations between characters. Be sure to review the punctuation rules on the use of quotation marks.

When you have finished your story, share it with your classmates by reading it aloud.

From *Notable Women*, by Arlene J. Morris-Lipsman, Copyright © 1990 Scott, Foresman and Company.

2. When she was younger, Louisa wrote plays that she and her sisters acted out. Imagine you are Louisa and write a play of your own.

Divide into small groups. Within your group, skim through the biography of Louisa May Alcott. Think about the many different adventures and experiences she lived through. Which ones are the most exciting to you?

Now, re-create Louisa's story by writing a short play about one of her experiences. As you write, include parts for Louisa's family or for people she met in her life. As you write speaking parts for your characters, try to imagine what they might have actually said and how they would have felt in the situation.

When you have finished writing your play, act it out using paper bag puppets as your characters. Draw faces and bodies for each character on brown or white paper bags. Stuff the bags with newspaper. Then staple them together at the bottom. Attach a stick or ruler to the bottom of each bag in order to support the puppets.

Now present your play to your classmates. You may want to disguise your voice as you play the parts of the different characters.

FOR FURTHER RESEARCH

1. Find out more about Louisa May Alcott's family and about American society during the 1860s by reading *Little Women*. Which characters seem especially real to you? Which events do you think might have actually occurred in Louisa's own life?

2. Louisa dreamed of being able to support her family. Her father, Bronson Alcott, a brilliant man, was simply unable to provide for his family. Find out more about Bronson Alcott, his unusual ideas, and how these ideas affected Louisa's early life.

3. Find out more about some of the other books Louisa wrote for children. How many books did she write? What were these books about? Were they as popular as *Little Women*?

FOR FURTHER READING

Meigs, Cornelia. *Invincible Louisa: The Story of the Author of "Little Women."* Boston: Little, Brown, 1933, 1961.

Papashvily, Helen Waite. *Louisa May Alcott*. Boston: Houghton Mifflin, 1965.

Pears, Catherine Owens. *Louisa May Alcott: Her Life*. New York: Holt, Rinehart and Winston, 1954.

Margaret Bourke-White

Photographer
1906–1971

N 1988 THE LIFE STORY OF MARGARET BOURKE-WHITE WAS TOLD in a television movie. Why would her life story make an interesting television drama?

For a few seconds, Margaret White glanced at her father's fine assortment of cameras. No, she decided, cameras were not especially interesting. And all during her childhood and teen years, Margaret never even took a picture.

While a student at Cornell University, however, Margaret was busily taking shots of the campus, and her fellow students were eagerly buying her pictures.

Nearing graduation, Margaret thought about her future. She had studied to be a biologist. However, the high praise she received for her photographic work convinced her to become a photographer.

For a while, Margaret Bourke-White (she was now using her middle name, which was also her mother's maiden name) worked as an architectural photographer. But she was already fascinated with America's industrial plants. Daring to enter what was considered a man's world, Margaret snapped shots of factories, heavy machinery, even steel in the making. By the time she was twenty-four, she had become one of America's leading industrial photographers.

Her talents led her to a job at *Fortune*, a magazine dedicated to business and industry. Traveling throughout the United States, even touring Russia, she eventually became a well-known photojournalist. Choosing her shots carefully, she told stories through pictures, with only a few accompanying words of explanation.

For Margaret Bourke-White, the industrial world was all that mattered—until 1934. In the mid-1930s, the American Midwest suffered a severe drought. Throughout the area, crops were ruined. Penniless farmers moved about the land, seeking work. Margaret, on an assignment to cover this "Dust Bowl," saw the despair of the people. How could she show this desperation so that others would understand, she wondered.

No longer interested in machinery and instead concerned about human beings, she traveled to the South. She would make others understand the horrors of poverty, she promised herself. Picture after picture, Margaret snapped away. Finally, in the late 1930s, she proudly presented her work to the American people. Her book, "You Have Seen Their Faces" (with text by her husband, Erskine Caldwell), simply and realistically showed the desperation of the poor. Her pictures touched the hearts of Americans everywhere.

Margaret was now in great demand as a photographer, and she was soon hired by *Life*, a magazine that told the news through pictures.

By 1941 the big news was World War II. Once again Margaret was in Russia, this time photographing the German attack on that country. Shooting from an open balcony outside her hotel room, with no thought to the danger she faced, Margaret captured the German bombing of Russia. Trudging onto battlefields, she caught the bitter retreat of the Russian soldiers.

For several months she stayed in Russia. Then, in late 1941, when the United States entered the war, Margaret was invited to work for the U.S. Air Force, the first woman to do so.

She went first to London, then to North Africa, where she became the first woman ever to fly on board a U.S. bombing mission. Then it was on to Italy, where she covered heavy fighting in that country. At last she reached Germany, and when the war was finally ended, Margaret took haunting pictures of Jewish war survivors.

Through her pictures, she had told her fellow Americans about the horrors of war. But there was another horror story she needed to tell. In 1959 she went to South Africa. Descending deep into the pits of the earth, Margaret shot pictures of the black men who were forced to work in South Africa's sweltering gold mines.

Four years later, in 1952, Margaret Bourke-White once again became a war correspondent, covering the Korean War. Hanging from a helicopter, flying high over town and country, Margaret snapped her shots.

She returned from Korea, eagerly looking forward to future assignments. But something was dreadfully wrong. A dull ache in her leg left her staggering when she walked, and her joints stiffened. Soon Margaret learned she was suffering from Parkinson's disease. After a long and courageous battle with her illness, Margaret Bourke-White died on August 27, 1971.

Like so many other women of her time, she could have taken a safer route—shooting portraits or perhaps even fashion. But that was not what Margaret cared to do. She understood the power of her pictures, the way they could tell a story. Willingly then, perhaps even eagerly, she faced danger. Margaret Bourke-White had, after all, many stories to tell.

FOR DISCUSSION

1. Why do you think Margaret found the industrial world so fascinating?

2. What do you think Margaret would consider the most important event in her life? How did that event affect her?

3. Why do you think the Air Force hired Margaret as a photographer?

4. Throughout her career, Margaret took haunting pictures of people suffering from poverty, war, and injustice. Given what you know about her, how do you think Margaret felt as she took these pictures? Explain your answer.

5. Are pictures as important as words, more important, or less important? Share your answer.

6. Why do photographers like Margaret Bourke-White take pictures of poverty, war, and injustice? Do you think it is necessary for photographers to take pictures of these horrors? Explain your answer.

QUOTABLE QUOTES

Margaret Bourke-White once said, "If you banish fear, nothing terribly bad can happen to you." As she lived her life, in what ways did she show she believed these words?

ACTIVITIES

1. Margaret Bourke-White wanted her pictures to express a certain message. As a result, she spent much time seeking an exact angle (position) from which to take her pictures. When she photographed people, she looked for facial expressions that would show specific emotions.

Imagine now that Margaret Bourke-White has come to your school to take pictures of the students. As usual, she is looking for a story to share with her audience.

In small groups, discuss what message or feeling you think Margaret would like to portray. Perhaps she would like to show students eagerly listening to their teacher. She may want to focus on one student in the group who is not quite paying attention. What else do you think Margaret might like to show?

Now arrange a photo scene Margaret might actually take. Within your corner of the room, arrange the furniture in a way that you think would make an interesting picture. Now decide where you will sit or stand, and think about your facial expressions. Will you smile? Will you be serious? Will you hold something in your hands?

When you have finished planning your scene, choose one person to act as Margaret Bourke-White. Now take your positions and wait for Margaret to take your picture.

From *Notable Women*, by Arlene J. Morris-Lipsman, Copyright © 1990 Scott, Foresman and Company.

If you are portraying Margaret, decide where you will stand to take the best picture. What will you say to the students as you take their picture? Now shoot the picture, using an imaginary camera—or, if you wish, a real one.

2. Margaret Bourke-White was a photojournalist. She told stories through pictures using only a few accompanying words of explanation. Imagine now that you, too, are a photojournalist. Look through several magazines and find four or five pictures (either in color or in black and white) that might fit together to make a short story. (Imagine that you have taken these pictures yourself.)

Now cut and paste the pictures on separate sheets of paper, and arrange them in order. Underneath each picture, write a few sentences that explain it. As you write, try to make sure your sentences tell a short, simple story.

Now make a book of your photographs, as Margaret often did, by placing a front cover over your pages. When you have finished, share your book with your classmates.

FOR FURTHER RESEARCH

1. Find out more about another woman photographer who lived when Margaret Bourke-White did, Dorothea Lange. In what ways was her work like Margaret's? In what ways was it different?

2. In your local library you will find books and magazines that tell stories through photographs. Ask your librarian to help you locate these photo essays. Look through these books or magazines and study the pictures. What story are these pictures telling? How do the pictures make you feel? Do the pictures help you to better understand the story?

3. The "Dust Bowl" of the 1930s changed Margaret Bourke-White's life. Find out more about the Dust Bowl. What actually happened? How did the Dust Bowl affect the people who lived through it? Why did the Dust Bowl affect Margaret the way it did?

FOR FURTHER READING

Gerah, Harry. *Women Who Made America Great*. Philadelphia: J. B. Lippincott, 1962, pp. 185–204.

Siegel, Beatrice. *An Eye on the World: Margaret Bourke-White, Photographer*. New York: Frederick Warne & Co., 1980.

THINKING IT OVER

1. Why do you think people living in the 1850s believed single young women belonged at home with their parents? How have attitudes toward young women changed over the years?

2. Compare the work of writers and photographers. In what ways do they both contribute to American society?

3. Louisa May Alcott and Margaret Bourke-White were both, in their own way, storytellers. In what ways did the content of their stories differ? Which woman do you think made a greater impact on American society? Explain your answer. Both women took risks in order to make their dreams come true. Compare and contrast the risks they took. Why do you think they were willing to take these risks?

AIR AND SPACE

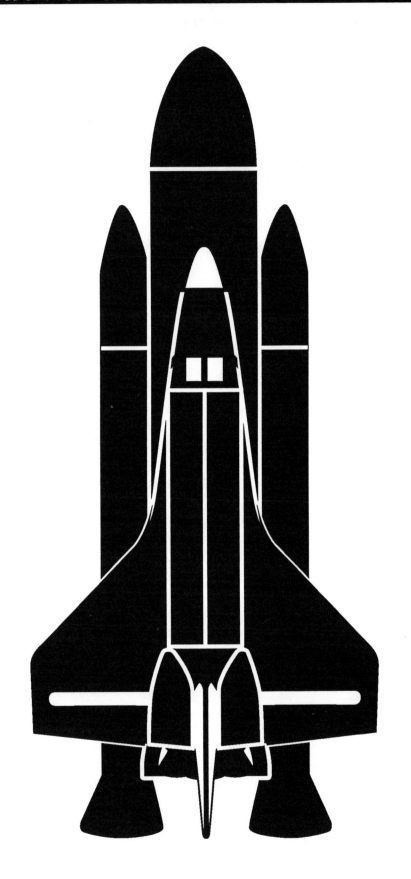

Amelia Earhart

Aviator
1897–1937

N 1928 AMELIA EARHART BECAME A NATIONAL HERO. However, she believed she was a false hero. In 1932, Amelia became satisfied that she was a true hero. What had Amelia done to prove to herself that she deserved her fame?

Eleven-year-old Amelia Earhart turned away from the airplane that was on display at the Iowa State Fair. In 1908 Amelia just wasn't interested in airplanes. Several years later, however, when she saw them in Toronto, Canada, they held her spellbound. And in 1920, when she took her first brief plane ride, Amelia Earhart knew she had to fly.

Taking lessons from experienced pilots, Amelia soon became an expert pilot herself. She was so skilled, in fact, that she bought her own plane when she was only twenty-five, using money she earned from various odd jobs.

At first, flying was only something to do for fun. Amelia needed to earn a living, so she began a career in social work. Then one day in 1928 she received a phone call that would change her life.

Amelia was invited to be a passenger on a transatlantic flight. If she agreed, she would become the first woman ever to cross the Atlantic by plane. Of course, Amelia said yes, and on June 16 the *Friendship* lifted off from Newfoundland, heading across the

From *Notable Women*, by Arlene J. Morris-Lipsman, Copyright © 1990 Scott, Foresman and Company.

Atlantic. Twenty hours and forty minutes later, the plane landed in Wales, and Amelia instantly became a worldwide heroine.

But Amelia was bothered by her fame. She had merely been a passenger. One day, she told herself, she would make the trip across the Atlantic alone, piloting her own plane. And on May 20, 1932 Amelia Earhart did just that. Taking off from Newfoundland, she flew across the Atlantic heading for Paris.

What a flight it was! She flew through storms, dense clouds, even ice. As for her plane, first her altimeter, which measured her height above land, broke. Then an exhaust pipe cracked and burst into flames. And Amelia also discovered a leak in her fuel line that sent fumes into the plane.

As a result, Amelia was forced to land in Ireland, not Paris. Despite that, the trip was a success. Amelia Earhart had become the first woman pilot to cross the Atlantic Ocean.

Now Amelia was really famous. She received many awards and honors. She also continued to set flying records—including becoming the first person to fly over the Pacific Ocean from Honolulu to California.

But Amelia Earhart wanted to do more. She wanted to fly around the world.

Eagerly she prepared for this flight, and at last she was ready. She would lift off from Miami and travel around the world at the equator, flying east to west.

Finally, on June 1, 1937, Amelia took off. Past South America, across Africa, on to India and Australia she flew, stopping along the way to repair her plane and to refuel. At last she reached New Guinea. One month had passed since takeoff, and all had gone well. Now all that remained was the flight from New Guinea to Howland Island in the Pacific for a refueling. Then it was on to Honolulu and back to America.

On July 2 Amelia left New Guinea headed for Howland Island. This would be the most dangerous part of her journey. Howland Island was just a tiny dot in the ocean. Unless her directions were accurate, she would miss it completely. United States ships waited in the waters below, their crews anxious to hear from her by radio, eager to guide her to the island.

However, Amelia contacted the waiting ships only a few times, and she didn't respond to any of the ship's signals to her. From her brief messages, it was clear that Amelia did not seem to be able to locate Howland Island. Even worse, she had reported that she was low on gas.

Desperately the ships sent out smoke signals, hoping to guide her down, but apparently Amelia did not see those signals. One final brief message came over the wires at 8:45 A.M. Then silence. Amelia Earhart was not heard from again.

Of course the ships searched for her. But neither Amelia nor her plane was ever found.

The American public was stunned by Amelia's disappearance, for they had come to love this independent, adventurous woman. Amelia Earhart, they knew, had lived life according to her own rules, not someone else's. Even though few women were entering the field, Amelia dared to be an aviator, for she believed that a woman was capable of pursuing any profession she chose.

When the search was finally called off sixteen days later, the American public sadly bid farewell to its beloved hero.

FOR DISCUSSION

1. In the beginning Amelia believed that flying was something just for fun. She never dreamed that flying would become her career. What happened to change her mind?

2. Even though Amelia would only be a passenger on the 1928 transatlantic flight, not the pilot, she agreed to go. Why do you think Amelia decided to make the flight?

3. Why do you think Amelia Earhart wanted to fly around the world?

4. Even though both Amelia's 1932 flight across the Atlantic and the flight around the world would be dangerous missions, she did not hesitate to go through with them. Why do you think Amelia was willing to risk her life to carry out these missions?

5. During her lifetime, Amelia Earhart set many different kinds of flying records. While male pilots were also setting records at this time, most of them never received the fame Amelia did. Why do you think this was so? Do you think it was fair to the male pilots? Explain your answer.

QUOTABLE QUOTES

About her last flight, Amelia said, "Please know that I am quite aware of the hazards. I want to do it because I want to do it. Women must try to do things as men have tried. When they fail, their failure must be but a challenge to others." What do these words tell you about Amelia's belief in women? In what ways did Amelia live her life by these words?

ACTIVITIES

1. Imagine that the year is 1928 and that you are Amelia Earhart. You have just returned to the United States after your famous flight across the Atlantic. The editor of a major magazine has asked you to write an article describing how you felt during those long hours aboard the *Friendship*.

Take a few moments to think about your feelings. How did you feel as you sat on the floor of the cold, dark plane? How did you feel when the plane's radio system failed to work? How did you feel as you flew through snow and rainstorms and strong winds? How did you feel when you finally landed in Wales? when you were treated as a celebrity?

Now write an article in which you describe your thoughts and feelings. Make your article as interesting as possible. Remember that it will be read by thousands of people.

When you have finished your articles, exchange them with a few of your classmates and share your thoughts. Then put all the articles together to make a book about Amelia Earhart.

2. During her lifetime, Amelia Earhart proved that she was a real hero. However, when she returned from her 1928 flight across the Atlantic, she herself did not feel that she deserved her fame. She had only been a passenger, she said.

Although some people agreed with her, others felt she deserved to be called a hero.

Imagine now that year is 1928 and that you are an editorial writer working for a

newspaper. (An editorial writer offers an opinion on a subject and backs it up with explanations that prove his or her point.) You are about to write an editorial article titled "Amelia Earhart—Hero or Not?" In your article state your opinion. Do you think Amelia is a hero? Then go on to explain why you feel as you do.

When you have finished, share your opinions with your classmates by reading your paper aloud.

FOR FURTHER RESEARCH

1. Amelia Earhart helped develop an organization just for women fliers. Find out more about some of the other early female fliers, such as Jacqueline Cochran and Ruth Nichols. Who were they? What did they do?

2. Find out more about Amelia's first flight across the Atlantic Ocean in 1928. What kinds of problems occurred on that flight? What dangers did Amelia face even though she was just a passenger?

3. Amelia loved planes, and if she were living today she would be amazed to see how they have changed over the years. Find out more about how planes have changed. Look through an encyclopedia or a book on airplanes and note the different models. Compare the first planes with today's superjets. What changes do you notice? After you have examined the planes, you may want to make a model of the one that interests you most. Bring your model to class to share it with your classmates.

FOR FURTHER READING

Brown, Fern G. *Amelia Earhart Takes Off*. Niles, Ill.: Albert Whitman & Company, 1985.

Genett, Ann. *Contributions of Women: Aviation*. Minneapolis, Minn.: Dillon Press, 1982, pp. 3–21.

Mondey, David. *Women of the Air*. Morristown, N.J.: Silver Burdett, 1982, pp. 5–19.

Randolph, Blythe. *Amelia Earhart*. New York: Franklin Watts, 1987.

Sally Ride

Astronaut
1951–

SALLY RIDE BECAME KNOWN TO ALL AS AN "AMERICAN FIRST." What did Sally Ride do to earn this reputation?

For young Sally Ride, playing baseball and football with the boys was simply a natural part of childhood. It didn't matter that she was often the only girl on an all-boys' team. She knew she could play as well as any boy.

By the time she was ten, however, she had developed a new interest, tennis. Because she played so well she was able to earn a partial scholarship to a private all-girls' high school.

In school Sally studied many things, but what fascinated her most was science. Even when she went on to college, she continued to study physics, a branch of science. But she still played tennis.

For a while, Sally was undecided. Should she choose a career in science or one in tennis? Finally, however, she reached a decision. She enrolled at Stanford University in California and eventually earned two degrees. One was in English; the other, of course, was in physics. Continuing her studies, Sally received both a master's and a doctorate degree in astrophysics, the science of stars and planets.

At last she was ready to look for a job. What would she do, she wondered? Then one day Sally read a newspaper advertisement that caught her attention. The National

Aeronautics and Space Administration (NASA), a training center for astronauts, was looking for men and women to fly on future space missions.

Sally Ride had never even thought about being an astronaut. Nor did she think about what it would mean to women if she were to become an astronaut. Suddenly, however, she knew she would answer this ad. She was one of more than eight thousand people who applied and one of one thousand women. But when NASA finally reached its decision in 1978, Sally Ride, along with thirty-four others, including five women, was selected to be an astronaut in training.

At the Johnson Space Center in Houston, Texas, Sally began to learn how to be an astronaut. There was so much to learn about—computers, the inside of a spacecraft, radio communication, parachute jumping. Sally even learned how to fly a jet. In addition, she also helped develop the huge mechanical robot arm that would be used to pick up satellites in orbit.

After completing her training, Sally worked as a capsule communicator for a while. From the ground, she radioed instructions to the crews aboard the spacecraft. Even though her job was important, and even though she was now married, Sally dreamed of something more. She wanted to fly in space.

Finally, in 1983, when she was thirty-two years old, she had the chance to do just that. She had been chosen to be part of a five-member crew that would fly aboard the spacecraft *Challenger*.

On *Challenger* she would serve as a mission specialist, working with the newly developed robot arm. She would also perform and check the scientific experiments that would be conducted in space.

Sally was confident that she would do her job well, but others wondered whether she would. After all, they said, she was a woman.

But she soon proved just how capable she could be. As a crowd of thousands watched the *Challenger* lift off on June 18, 1983, Sally was ready. As the spacecraft orbited the earth every ninety minutes, sixteen times in one day, Sally carefully carried out her assignments.

For six days, she lived aboard the spacecraft. Finally, when all the experiments had been completed, the *Challenger* returned to earth, landing on the Mojave Desert in California.

A year later, Sally was back in space, this time on an eight-day mission. How she looked forward to her third mission aboard the *Challenger*, scheduled for July 1986.

However, in January 1986 a terrible accident occurred. The *Challenger* exploded after lifting off, killing all the astronauts aboard. What caused this explosion, people wondered? Sally Ride was the only astronaut appointed to serve on the investigating commission to find out. This was her last public role as an astronaut. A short while later, Sally Ride announced her retirement from NASA.

As an astronaut, she had held the country spellbound. She was, after all, an American pioneer. The nation had cheered her on, applauding her courage. And when she had emerged from the spacecraft *Challenger* after her first mission, a great cheer rose throughout the country. Sally Ride had become the first American woman to fly in space.

FOR DISCUSSION

1. Until she saw the advertisement in the paper, Sally had never considered a job as an astronaut. Why do you think this was so?

2. What qualifications do you think Sally must have had to be selected as an astronaut-in-training?

3. Because she was a woman, some people wondered whether she would be able to perform her duties in space. Why do you suppose they felt this way? If you were to meet any of these people, what would you say to them?

4. Why do you think Sally retired from NASA?

5. Why do you think Sally was the only astronaut chosen to serve on the commission that investigated the *Challenger* explosion?

QUOTABLE QUOTES

George W. S. Abbey, director of flight operations for NASA, once said, "Sally Ride is smart in a very special way. You get people who can sit in the lab and think like an Einstein, but they can't do anything with it. Sally can get everything she knows together and bring it to bear where you need it." What do these words mean? Who was Einstein? Based on this description of her, why do you think Sally made a good astronaut?

ACTIVITIES

1. Many people are curious about space. What is space like, they wonder. Sally Ride had the opportunity to find out when she rode the *Challenger* into space. What kinds of things do you think Sally saw as she orbited the earth?

Divide the class into small groups. In your group, draw, paint, or cut and paste a space scene on a large sheet of paper. Before you create your picture, discuss what kinds of things you will include in it—things Sally might have seen. Use your imagination and include as many creative and interesting sights as possible.

When you have finished your pictures, look through your Language Arts book or a book on poetry and find out about a form of poetry called the cinquain. Now look at your picture once again. Write a cinquain to describe your space scene.

After you have completed your cinquain, attach it to your picture and display your projects around the room.

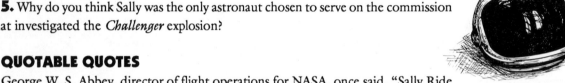

2. Sally Ride first learned about the space program by reading an advertisement in the newspaper. Newspapers are one way of advertising. Television commercials are another. Think about some of the television commercials you have seen. Which are your favorites? What makes these commercials interesting to you? Within your classroom, discuss the qualities that make an interesting commercial. List your ideas on the chalkboard.

Now divide into small groups. Within your group, create a television advertisement to interest people in becoming a part of the space program. How many people will you use to act out the commercials? What will each person say? Write a short script for your advertisement. Will you sing a song in your commercial? Think of a song you like. Use that melody and make up words of your own about the space program. Will you use posters as part of your advertisement? What else will you use?

When you have finished making up your commercial, practice it. Then present it to your classmates.

FOR FURTHER RESEARCH

1. Find out more about another famous woman astronaut, Judy Resnick. In what ways was Judy like Sally Ride? What happened to Judy Resnick?

2. Find out more about some of NASA's current space research programs. What are space scientists trying to learn about? What research programs are currently being sponsored by NASA? How are these programs similar to or different from the ones Sally Ride participated in?

3. Find out about our country's space history. When did the first space mission occur? What was accomplished? How many astronauts were involved? Who were they? Learn about some of the other early space missions. Which ones were successful? Were there any other space tragedies besides the Challenger explosion? How were the early missions similar to or different from the ones Sally Ride participated in?

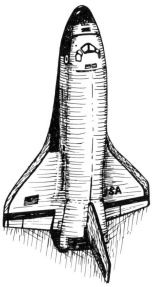

FOR FURTHER READING

Behrens, June. *Sally Ride, Astronaut: An American First*. Chicago: Childrens Press, 1984.

O'Connor, Karen. *Sally Ride and the New Astronauts: Scientists in Space*. New York: Franklin Watts, 1983.

Ride, Sally, with Susan Okie. *To Space and Back*. New York: Lothrop, Lee & Shepard, 1986.

THINKING IT OVER

1. Do you think it is important for women to be chosen to serve on space missions? Explain your answer.

2. What lessons can we, as a nation, learn from such tragedies as the disappearance of Amelia Earhart and the explosion of *Challenger*?

3. Amelia Earhart and Sally Ride both "took to the skies." In what ways did these women face similar challenges and risks? Which woman do you think faced more challenges as she sought to advance her career? Explain your answer.

4. In what ways did both Amelia and Sally help make advances in the field of air and space? Who do you think contributed more to the field? Explain your answer.

Mildred Didrikson Zaharias

Athlete
1911–1956

FROM THE TIME SHE WAS A HIGH SCHOOL STUDENT, Babe Didrikson Zaharias amazed Americans with her spectacular abilities. For what did her fans admire Babe?

Another baseball game, thought eleven-year-old Mildred Didrikson. Another chance to prove that she was a champ. Mildred paused in her thoughts, then smiled proudly for a moment. She was thinking about her newest nickname—Babe. And like the great baseball hero Babe Ruth, Babe Didrikson could wallop a ball.

Baseball, rollerskating, swimming, diving—it didn't matter what the sport was. Babe loved them all. And she played them all well, too. Young Babe, in fact, already dreamed of the day when she would be the world's greatest athlete.

By the time Babe was in high school, her interest had turned to basketball. Joining the girls' basketball team, Babe soon proved she was no ordinary player. No, Babe was the star. And before she had even graduated, Babe was invited to join the Golden Cyclones of Dallas, a basketball team of young working women. Now, in game after game, Babe led her new team to victory.

But playing basketball was only part of Babe's dream. As a teenager, she had been fascinated by stories of the 1928 Olympic Games. She had promised herself then that she would compete as a track star in the next Olympics.

From *Notable Women*, by Arlene J. Morris-Lipsman, Copyright © 1990 Scott, Foresman and Company.

In 1932, when the Olympic tryouts were held, Babe was ready. She entered eight competitions and won five. More important, she had won a position on the United States Olympic track team.

How excited she was! She would be participating in three events. When the 1932 games were held, Babe won two gold medals. Even more, she had broken two world records—for javelin throwing and for the hurdles race. Throughout the United States, newspapers screamed out the story of the fabulous Babe Didrikson.

For a while, Babe could hardly wait to prove herself again in the 1936 Olympic Games. But by 1933 she had decided to become a professional sports star instead of an amateur. (A professional receives money for participating in sports events, while an amateur does not.) As a professional, she was ineligible to participate in the Olympics. So Babe instead toured the country showing off her sports skills.

Babe soon discovered that she missed amateur competition sports. So she decided that she would learn to play golf. She would become the best woman golfer in the nation, she promised herself. And that's exactly what happened. Babe won the second golf tournament she ever played and was on her way to becoming a champ once more.

Suddenly, however, Babe's dreams came crashing down. The United States Golf Association ruled that she was a professional and ineligible to play in amateur golf tournaments. Babe had only one choice if she wanted to play amateur golf. For three years she must accept no money for her sports appearances. And that's what she did. Finally, in 1943 Babe Didrikson Zaharias (she had married George Zaharias in 1938) was ready to resume her career.

Now she astounded audiences with her golfing skills. In one year, from 1946 to 1947, Babe played tournament after tournament, winning an unheard of seventeen in a row. She even became the first American woman to win the British Women's Amateur tournament. She was indeed the champ. Time after time, she was named Woman Athlete of the Year by America's sports writers.

By 1953, though, something was terribly wrong with Babe. Severe pain left her back aching and too weak for her to play well. When she finally saw a doctor, his diagnosis was cancer.

The newspapers predicted that she would never play golf again. But a determined Babe was back swinging her golf clubs just three and a half months after surgery. A year later, she thrilled her fans by winning several major tournaments.

It seemed as though nothing could stop Babe, not even cancer. But in 1955, sadly, the cancer returned, leaving Babe too weak to pick up her clubs. A short while later, on September 27, 1956, the great champion died.

Throughout her sports career, Babe had amazed her fans. First as an Olympic star, she had captured her audience's hearts. Later, as a golfer, she left a winning record unmatched by any other woman. No wonder, then, that even before her death she was being called the greatest woman athlete of the first half of the twentieth century.

FOR DISCUSSION

1. Why do you think Babe, more than anything else, wanted to compete in the 1932 Olympics?

2. Why do you think Babe gave up a chance at the 1936 Olympics, choosing instead to become a professional athlete?

3. Even though Babe had never played professional golf, why do you think the United States Golf Association ruled her a professional? Do you think this was fair? Explain your answer.

QUOTABLE QUOTES

Although she was battling cancer, Babe Didrikson Zaharias refused to retire from sports. As she explained it, "One reason that I don't retire is that every time I get out and play well in a tournament it seems to encourage people with the same trouble I had." What do you think Babe meant? In what ways could Babe encourage others by continuing to play?

ACTIVITIES

1. During her lifetime, Babe Didrikson Zaharias played many sports, and she played them all well. In some ways her sports career was like a collage—a variety of pieces of pictures pasted on one large sheet of paper.

A collage is also a piece of art. In your classroom, make a collage to represent Babe's career. On a large sheet of paper, paste pictures or objects that represent all the sports you think Babe might have played. You may use actual pictures or you may create sports objects yourself. Use as many different materials as you wish —magazine pictures, aluminum foil, paste sticks, rubber bands, for example. Think about other materials that you would like to use and about what you will make.

When you have all your items, paste them on the paper in any position you wish. They do not have to be straight up and down, nor do they have to be in one certain order.

When you have finished your collage, title it. Then display it with others around the room.

2. As a sports star, Babe Didrikson Zaharias may have received many letters from her fans, especially from young students. What do you think these letters might have said?

Imagine that you lived when Babe did and that you read about her in the newspapers or actually saw her perform a sport. You are a fan of Babe's and you have decided to write her a letter. What will you say? Will you tell her about yourself? You may want to tell her about your favorite sport and why you like it. Think about what else you will say.

Now write your letter. Be sure to use the proper form for writing a friendly letter. When you have finished your letter, share it with classmates by reading it aloud.

From *Notable Women*, by Arlene J. Morris-Lipsman, Copyright © 1990 Scott, Foresman and Company.

FOR FURTHER RESEARCH

1. The Olympics have been played for many years. Find out more about some other women Olympic stars, such as Sonja Heine or Olga Korbut. In what ways were their careers similar to Babe's? In what ways were they different?

2. Find out more about the game of golf, the sport Babe loved. How is it played? What skills are required in order to play the game well? How is golf different from some of the sports you play?

3. Find out more about women's golf tournaments. Who are some of today's champion women golfers? Do their records match Babe's? Would you say that Babe Didrikson Zaharias still ranks as America's top woman golfer?

FOR FURTHER READING

Ryan, Joan. *Contributions of Women: Sports*. Minneapolis, Minn.: Dillon Press, 1975, pp. 7–27.

Schoor, Gene. *Babe Didrikson: The World's Greatest Woman Athlete*. Garden City, N.Y.: Doubleday & Company, 1978.

Smith, Beatrice S. *The Babe: Mildred Didrikson Zaharias*. Milwaukee, Wisc.: Raintree Editions, 1976.

Wilma Rudolph

Olympic Star
1940–

WHEN SHE WAS A CHILD, no one would have predicted that Wilma Rudolph would become a world-famous athlete. She faced a handicap that prevented her from living a normal childhood. Against what handicap did Wilma battle?

Blanche Rudolph gazed at her four-and-a-half-pound newborn daughter. Wilma was so tiny, so delicate. Would she even live, Mrs. Rudolph wondered?

Despite her mother's fears, Wilma Rudolph did survive. But by the time she was four, her young life was in danger once more. She was stricken first with double pneumonia, then with scarlet fever. Close to death, Wilma slowly began to recover, but sadly she did not regain full health. Her left leg had become paralyzed, leaving her unable to walk.

The doctors offered a little hope. Perhaps, they told Mrs. Rudolph, Wilma might one day walk again if she underwent therapy and if her legs were massaged daily.

Once a week, then, for the next two years, Mrs. Rudolph, determined that Wilma would walk again, made the forty-five mile trip to Nashville, Tennessee where Wilma received special treatments. And at home she taught her other children how to massage Wilma's legs.

When she was eight, Wilma began to wear a heavy metal brace. It was uncomfortable, but now at least she could move about. The brace was soon replaced by a special corrective shoe, and by the time Wilma was eleven she had beaten her handicap. She could walk on her own.

Wilma Rudolph did more than walk, however. Enthusiastically she played basketball with her brothers and sisters. Basketball was her favorite sport, and when she entered high school, Wilma eagerly joined the girls' team. Wilma soon proved she could play well. In fact, she set a Tennessee state record for girls by scoring 803 points in twenty-five games.

But Wilma soon discovered she could run even better than she could play basketball. As a member of the track team, she never lost a race, and in 1956, much to her surprise, fifteen-year-old Wilma Rudolph found she had qualified for a position on the United States Olympic Track Team.

Off she went to Melbourne, Australia, her hopes high. But 1956 was not the big year for Wilma Rudolph. She won only one third place (bronze) medal.

In 1957 Wilma graduated from high school and began college. Of course, she was a member of the track team. How she looked forward to competing! But once again poor health put Wilma on the sidelines. She sat out for the 1958 season, too sick to run, and in 1959 she pulled a muscle in her left thigh. A year later, she was severly ill after an operation to remove her tonsils.

Despite it all, Wilma Rudolph would not give up. After practicing whenever she could, in 1960 she once again earned a place on the United States Olympic Track Team.

Perhaps the other Olympic stars were nervous, but not Wilma. She thrilled the audiences, winning the 100- and 200-meter dashes. She also led her team to victory in the 400-meter relay race. As the 1960 Olympic Games ended, Wilma Rudolph calmly accepted her gold medals. Proudly, she realized she had become the first American woman ever to receive three gold medals.

The delighted crowds screamed their approval. Wherever she went—through Europe competing in meets or back in the United States—Wilma Rudolph was a celebrity. Just as important, she was also named Woman Athlete of the Year.

Wilma was back competing the following year. She participated in the Millrose Games (usually an all-male sporting event) and easily won a special 60-yard dash for women. Again and again, she ran and won—in New York, Louisville, even Germany. Again and again, she set world records.

The honors kept pouring in, too. In 1961 she won the Sullivan Memorial Trophy as the best amateur athlete, the third woman and the first black woman to do so. In 1962 she won the Babe Didrikson Zaharias Award as outstanding woman athlete of the world.

Her fans had hoped to see her perform again in the 1964 Olympics, but Wilma had made a different decision. She retired from amateur sports—a champion to the American public. Now this great American athlete looked forward to conquering other worlds.

Even though Wilma Rudolph had hung up her track shoes, to her adoring fans she would always be known as the speediest woman runner in the world.

FOR DISCUSSION

1. How do you think young Wilma felt when she received the bronze medal in the 1956 Olympic Games? Explain your answer.

2. Why do you think Wilma did not give up despite her many illnesses?

3. Even when she was about to participate in a race, Wilma was never nervous. Why do you think this was so? What makes you nervous? What things can we do to help control our nervousness?

4. What valuable lessons do you think Wilma might have learned from her mother?

5. Although Wilma was at the height of her sports career, she made the decision to retire. Why do you think she did this?

QUOTABLE QUOTES

After her retirement, Wilma devoted herself to teaching and giving sports demonstrations to children in ghetto cities. Thinking about her decision to retire, Wilma said, "I've been asked to run as a pro, but my interests now are my family . . . and the kids I'm working with. Now I'm trying to develop other champions." Why do you think Wilma wants to help others achieve success?

ACTIVITIES

1. The Olympics are one of the greatest sports events in the world. Adults and children enjoy watching Olympic competitions on television.

Imagine that you and your classmates are Olympic stars like Wilma Rudolph, and imagine that the Olympics are being held in your own classroom.

As a class, talk about, then list, some competitions that you can perform safely in your classroom. These do not have to be actual Olympic sports. Instead, you may make up competitions of your own. You can list events to be performed either by teams or by individuals. When you have completed your list, as a class choose three or four events that seem most interesting to you.

Now conduct an "Olympics" in your classroom by performing the competitions on your list. At the end of each competition be sure to show good sportsmanship by congratulating the winners.

2. Using an encyclopedia or a book about sports, find out about some of the competitions that make up the summer Olympics. List these events on the chalkboard and discuss them. Talk about what sports skills are involved, what the Olympic stars might wear, and what kind of equipment they would use.

Now make an Olympics mural for your classroom. First choose an Olympic sport that is most interesting to you. Next, take several large pieces of finger-painting paper taped together or a large sheet of brown wrapping paper and tape it across the chalkboard or wall of your classroom. Choose a space on the paper and paint or draw an Olympic scene that tells something about the sport you have chosen.

When the mural is finished, walk past it from beginning to end so that you can see every Olympic scene.

FOR FURTHER RESEARCH

1. Find out more about the history of the Olympics. When did the games begin? How often are they played? Which nations participate in the Olympics?

2. Find out more about the sport of track. What skills are required in order to perform well? What types of competitions do track stars compete in?

3. Find out more about some of today's American women who have partici-pated in the Olympic games. Have they broken any records? How many medals have they won? How has their performance compared to Wilma Rudolph's?

FOR FURTHER READING

Davis, Mac. *Pacemakers in Track and Field.* Cleveland: World Publishing Company, 1968, pp. 90–93.

Moffett, Martha. *Great Women Athletes.* New York: Platt & Munk, 1974, pp. 60–63.

Ryan, Joan. Contributions of Women: Sports. Minneapolis, Minn.: Dillon Press, 1975, pp. 47–63.

THINKING IT OVER

1. Why do you think professional athletes are ineligible to participate in the Olympics? Do you think this is fair? Explain your answer.

2. Why do you think that nations throughout the world participate in the Olympic Games?

3. Some people feel that competition sports are not very important. Do you feel this way? Explain your answer.

4. Compare the careers of Babe Didrikson Zaharias and Wilma Rudolph. Both women faced obstacles as they tried to achieve victory in the sports world. Which woman do you think faced the more serious obstacles? Explain your answer.

SUMMING IT UP

**COMPARISON
CHART:
SUMMING
IT UP**

Complete the charts on the following pages for each woman you read about. After you have filled in the spaces, read the following questions. Write a brief answer to each. Be prepared to discuss your answers with your classmates.

1. Think about the obstacles all of these women faced in their lives. Some of them faced fewer obstacles than others. Why do you think this was so?

2. Think about the lives of these notable women. Now think about the lives of some notable women you yourself know. Have they faced serious opposition as they've pursued their career goals? Do you think attitudes toward career women have changed over the years? Explain your answer. If you think attitudes have changed, why do you think this is so?

	WHERE AND WHEN SHE LIVED	PERSONAL QUALITIES	OBSTACLES SHE FACED	SIGNIFICANT CONTRIBUTIONS
Golda Meir				

	WHERE AND WHEN SHE LIVED	PERSONAL QUALITIES	OBSTACLES SHE FACED	SIGNIFICANT CONTRIBUTIONS
Indira Gandhi				

	WHERE AND WHEN SHE LIVED	PERSONAL QUALITIES	OBSTACLES SHE FACED	SIGNIFICANT CONTRIBUTIONS
Margaret Thatcher				

	WHERE AND WHEN SHE LIVED	PERSONAL QUALITIES	OBSTACLES SHE FACED	SIGNIFICANT CONTRIBUTIONS
Sandra Day O'Connor				

From *Notable Women*, by Arlene J. Morris-Lipsman, Copyright © 1990 Scott, Foresman and Company.

110

	WHERE AND WHEN SHE LIVED	PERSONAL QUALITIES	OBSTACLES SHE FACED	SIGNIFICANT CONTRIBUTIONS
Benazir Bhutto				

	WHERE AND WHEN SHE LIVED	PERSONAL QUALITIES	OBSTACLES SHE FACED	SIGNIFICANT CONTRIBUTIONS
Maria Mitchell				

From *Notable Women*, by Arlene J. Morris-Lipsman, Copyright © 1990 Scott, Foresman and Company.

	WHERE AND WHEN SHE LIVED	PERSONAL QUALITIES	OBSTACLES SHE FACED	SIGNIFICANT CONTRIBUTIONS
Marie Curie				

	WHERE AND WHEN SHE LIVED	PERSONAL QUALITIES	OBSTACLES SHE FACED	SIGNIFICANT CONTRIBUTIONS
Sylvia Earle				

112

	WHERE AND WHEN SHE LIVED	PERSONAL QUALITIES	OBSTACLES SHE FACED	SIGNIFICANT CONTRIBUTIONS
Susan B. Anthony				

	WHERE AND WHEN SHE LIVED	PERSONAL QUALITIES	OBSTACLES SHE FACED	SIGNIFICANT CONTRIBUTIONS
Harriet Tubman				

	WHERE AND WHEN SHE LIVED	PERSONAL QUALITIES	OBSTACLES SHE FACED	SIGNIFICANT CONTRIBUTIONS
Jane Addams				

	WHERE AND WHEN SHE LIVED	PERSONAL QUALITIES	OBSTACLES SHE FACED	SIGNIFICANT CONTRIBUTIONS
Mary McLeod Bethune				

	WHERE AND WHEN SHE LIVED	PERSONAL QUALITIES	OBSTACLES SHE FACED	SIGNIFICANT CONTRIBUTIONS
Eleanor Roosevelt				

	WHERE AND WHEN SHE LIVED	PERSONAL QUALITIES	OBSTACLES SHE FACED	SIGNIFICANT CONTRIBUTIONS
Mother Teresa				

	WHERE AND WHEN SHE LIVED	PERSONAL QUALITIES	OBSTACLES SHE FACED	SIGNIFICANT CONTRIBUTIONS
Betty Friedan				

	WHERE AND WHEN SHE LIVED	PERSONAL QUALITIES	OBSTACLES SHE FACED	SIGNIFICANT CONTRIBUTIONS
Elizabeth Blackwell				

116

	WHERE AND WHEN SHE LIVED	PERSONAL QUALITIES	OBSTACLES SHE FACED	SIGNIFICANT CONTRIBUTIONS
Florence Nightingale				

	WHERE AND WHEN SHE LIVED	PERSONAL QUALITIES	OBSTACLES SHE FACED	SIGNIFICANT CONTRIBUTIONS
Louisa May Alcott				

	WHERE AND WHEN SHE LIVED	PERSONAL QUALITIES	OBSTACLES SHE FACED	SIGNIFICANT CONTRIBUTIONS
Margaret Bourke-White				

	WHERE AND WHEN SHE LIVED	PERSONAL QUALITIES	OBSTACLES SHE FACED	SIGNIFICANT CONTRIBUTIONS
Amelia Earhart				

118

	WHERE AND WHEN SHE LIVED	PERSONAL QUALITIES	OBSTACLES SHE FACED	SIGNIFICANT CONTRIBUTIONS
Sally Ride				

	WHERE AND WHEN SHE LIVED	PERSONAL QUALITIES	OBSTACLES SHE FACED	SIGNIFICANT CONTRIBUTIONS
Mildred Didrikson Zaharias				

From *Notable Women*, by Arlene J. Morris-Lipsman, Copyright © 1990 Scott, Foresman and Company.